"Wally Kroeker not only hits the nail on the head; he drives it past the knots of our hearts into the soft wood of our souls. Wally shares, prods, nudges, budges, and even tickles us out of our pews into an attitude of service. I, for one, am encouraged to be reminded."
—*Dan Quisenberry, Poet, Former Major League Baseball Pitcher*

"Like a fast-stepping, fun-loving fighter, Wally Kroeker with inimitable style keeps delivering the punches: There are no secular jobs for Christians. Work at any job is a ministry. Christians are God's double agents, infiltrating the work of the world. He calls us to treat the marketplace as a launchpad for missions."
—*Katie Funk Wiebe, Author*

"I really like this stuff. An excellent contribution to applied faith."
—*Pete Hammond, in the Foreword*

God's Week Has 7 Days

Monday
Musings
for
Marketplace
Christians

Wally Kroeker

Herald
Press

Waterloo, Ontario
Scottdale, Pennsylvania

Canadian Cataloguing-in-Publication Data
Kroeker, Wally, 1946-
  God's week has seven days : Monday musings for market-
place Christians

ISBN 0-8361-9096-3

1. Work—Religious aspects—Christianity. 2. Business ethics.
3. Christian ethics. I. Title.

BY738.5.K76 1998   248.8'8   C98-931342-5

The paper used in this publication is recycled and meets the mini-
mum requirements of the American National Standard for Information Sciences—Permanence of Paper for Printed Library Materials,
ANSI Z39.48-1984.

GOD'S WEEK HAS SEVEN DAYS
Copyright © 1998 by Herald Press, Waterloo, Ont. N2L 6H7
  Published simultaneously in USA by Herald Press,
  Scottdale, Pa. 15683. All rights reserved
Canadiana Entry Number: C98-931342-5
Library of Congress Catalog Card Number: 98-72453
International Standard Book Number: 0-8361-9096-3
Printed in the United States of America
Interior and cover art by Matthew C. Eberly
Book and cover design by Gwen M. Stamm

07 06 05 04 03 02 01 00 99 98 10 9 8 7 6 5 4 3 2 1

To my dear Millie,
whose faith has seven days

Contents

Foreword by Pete Hammond 10
Preface 13

JANUARY
    What? Not again? .17
    Write your own obit? 20
    If Jesus came to the office 23
    Second-mile service 26
    Daddy, would you write for *Playboy*? 29

FEBRUARY
    Getting it together 35
    The Bible at your desk 38
    God's double agents 41
    Thawing out frozen assets 44

MARCH
    With friends like these 49
    Lighten up 52
    Little white anecdotes 55
    Rules of the game 58

APRIL
    Kicking the bag 63
    Waddling down unfriendly aisles 66
    Shy about God? 69
    Which type is your company? 72

MAY

    Death and revenue enhancement 77

    In praise of small steps 80

    Rush to judgment 83

    Get a whiff of this 86

    The business of theology 89

JUNE

    At play in the Word of the Lord 95

    Who is my neighbor? 98

    Lord of the hoeing 101

    Why Otis stayed unsaved 104

JULY

    A gospel of grit .109

    Power in the hands of a few 112

    Grocery graces .115

    Nothing without love 118

AUGUST

    Sewage ethics 123

    Me? A bleeding heart? 126

    Shall we whine together? 129

    Business—a mixed blessing 132

    How green is my job? 135

SEPTEMBER

    We care about the work you do 141

    Soiling the brain 144

    Potato pride 147

    An executive worth his salt 150

OCTOBER

    First-aid ethics 155

    The Monday connection 158

    A hiding place of gray 161

    The CEO as pastor 164

NOVEMBER

    A hand of welcome 169

    Blueprint from above 172

    Explosive profit .175

    What if . . . ? 178

DECEMBER

    What's the real cost? 183

    Oom-pah-pah 186

    Do you hear what I hear? 189

    A parable of rude awakening 192

    Shaping up 195

The Author 197

MEDA: Mennonite Economic
    Development Associates 199

Foreword

I am delighted to have Wally Kroeker's wisdom in a package that can travel far beyond the circulation of the *Marketplace* periodical published by Mennonite Economic Development Associates (MEDA). Wally writes as a realist with the gift of lively candor salted down with healthy humor.

These reflections range far and wide across the church's deep need for more connections between our faith and everyday life. Wally touches on basic flaws in our worship experiences that tend to exclude God from daily work. He probes the frequently mentioned but seldom helped gray areas of workplace relations, decisions, routines, negotiations, and dilemmas.

Wally is much more than a good journalist and writer. He has slugged it out in the ever-challenging roles of being a Christian as a university student, employee in agribusiness, professional journalist, husband, dad, grandpa, and long-term member of the MEDA team. Along this journey, he has regularly listened carefully to associates and reflected on what it means to love and serve Jesus Christ in such contexts.

This can be a lonely road. The church of North

America has often not made good-faith connections with the areas of work, citizenship, and daily relationships. Only in recent years are new stirrings surfacing on these issues. We are seeing the beginning of a new era in which the daily application of faith is emerging as a major new agenda.

Christians are challenging the old ways of faith as a Sunday-only experience, with occasional bursts of interest in world missions. In the last twenty years, they are giving fresh attention to what believers face in daily life. On such matters, we have seen a steady flow of new books, publications, videos, seminars, and workshops, and a growing number of sermons and Bible studies.

This development of daily discipleship might be just in time. The young generation is demonstrating its impatience with compartmentalized faith. They are hungering for a more seamless and integral experience with Jesus Christ.

Wally's reflections fit right into this stirring within believers. He invites his readers to a year of weekly engagement on faith that shapes how we work in government, healthcare, business, education, food production, and economics. And he does it with a compelling style. His wit, personal vulnerability, and agonizing realism are right on target.

I admit that I really like this stuff and want many others to taste and see that the Lord is *very* concerned with the routines and challenges of our workplaces in homes, companies, schools, farms, and the halls of government. Jesus is Lord of every element of creation, and he longs for us to follow him in every activity of daily life. This book is an excellent contribution to that exercise.

Join me in figuring out which of our Christian friends and seekers of spirituality should receive this gift of applied faith.

—*Pete Hammond*
  Developer of the Word in Life Study Bible
  Presbyterian Church (USA) Elder
  Ministry-in-Daily-Life Leader,
  InterVarsity Christian Fellowship
  Madison, Wisconsin

Preface

When I was a child, I learned that God worked six days and then took one day off. By the time I got into the workforce, something had changed. God owned the Lord's Day, and the rest were ours—five for our jobs and one for yard work.

A few years into my career, I began to wonder if I was being called to "Christian service." To me, that meant working for a religious organization. It never occurred to me that being a "secular" journalist could qualify as Christian service.

When I joined the staff of a Christian magazine in central Kansas, I was somehow thought to be in the "Lord's work," while my neighbors—farmers, store clerks, real estate agents—were not. I would serve the Lord from eight to five; they would have to wait till after five. I was called, they were hired.

It took many years for me to grasp that all our work is service to God, and as such, is equal in value. As the Reformer William Tyndale said, "There is no work better than another to please God; to pour water, to wash dishes, to be a cobbler, or an apostle."

I had grown up in a church committed to "the priesthood of all believers." So I should have known that wherever I worked, God was there, wanting me to "press the kingdom" into my daily tasks and relationships.

A good part of this journey of awareness took place when I became editor of *The Marketplace*, a magazine for Christians in business. It is published by Mennonite Economic Development Associates, an organization committed to the integration of Christian faith, business, and economic development. Neil Janzen, then president of MEDA, encouraged me to reflect and write about the grace notes we find between our work and our faith.

The thoughts that follow represent part of my journey to see the workplace as an arena of spiritual activity. Many of these pieces appeared in different form in *The Marketplace*. Some were written when I was editor of *The Christian Leader*, the magazine of the U.S. Mennonite Brethren Conference.

I do not claim to present a seamless garment or a comprehensive theology of daily ministry. These are Monday morning musings (one for each week), snippets of life seen through the lens of Christian faith. They highlight some areas where faith, ethics, obedience, compassion, and community intersect with the world of daily work and commerce.

The Christian life goes far beyond Sunday. All the days of the week belong to God.

—*Wally Kroeker*
  Editor, The Marketplace
  Winnipeg, Canada

January

What? Not again?

It's January, and unless you're a retail merchant, you've likely had enough of Christmas. The tree has been composted; the crèche set put away. You may be glad it's over for another year.

Where I live, Christmas is big. My city calls itself "the Christmas Capital." A lot of religiosity comes out of hiding. Suddenly people who otherwise show little sign of being religious are excited about the incarnation of God's Son.

It's a much bigger celebration than Easter. Community and business life pays a lot of attention to Christmas, but skips easily over Easter.

Maybe that's because Christmas is so sanitized. The stable is clean, the livestock are house-trained, and the swaddling clothes are bleached-white. The baby Jesus is easy to take: cuddly, quiet, no threat.

Easter's not as much fun. Well, Easter Sunday is great, but Good Friday? We're not really turned on by the cross.

We also manage to move speedily between the two seasons. In our haste to celebrate the beginning and end of Christ's life on earth, we miss the period when Jesus really showed what the kingdom of God looks like on a daily basis. We miss the Monday-to-

Friday of God's week.

I used to attend a church where the Apostles' Creed was recited every Sunday: "I believe in God the Father Almighty, Maker of heaven and earth: and in Jesus Christ his only Son our Lord, who was conceived by the Holy Spirit, born of the Virgin Mary, suffered under Pontius Pilate. . . ."

It's an important theological statement, but it moves too fast. There's only a comma between "born of the Virgin Mary" and "suffered under Pontius Pilate."

In between, we miss the entire life and teachings of Jesus. We miss all those clues telling us how he wants us to act in the workplaces where we spend some of our best hours. The comma doesn't really do justice to the fact that in his day-to-day life, Jesus was the clearest expression of what God is like and what God intends for us.

It's the grown-up Jesus who says, "Follow me." It's the grown-up Jesus who makes troubling demands of us and says unsettling things about preaching good news to the poor and proclaiming liberty to the oppressed. It's the grown-up Jesus who gives us courage to be "salt and light" in our daily work.

We've celebrated Christmas just a few weeks ago. In a few months, we'll celebrate Easter. We remember the birth, death, and resurrection of our Lord.

God's year also calls us to celebrate the time in between, when Jesus preached, healed, and taught.

It's an important time, this interval between Christmas and Easter. Without it we can't really understand Jesus or truly know him.

This is the time when we carry out the work he gave us—"As the Father has sent me, I am sending you" (John 20:21, NIV). This is the time that defines our mission in the workplace as "ministers of commerce."

May our Christmas last a little longer.

May it last until Easter.

Write your own obit?

A young friend was surprised to hear that I usually scan the obituaries in our local newspaper.

"Weird," the friend said. "You must be getting old."

I suppose so. More of the older generation, including my peers' parents and some former colleagues, are showing up on the obituary page.

In addition, that's the page where I cut my teeth in the newspaper business. My first writing job was with a midsized daily where a person's passing was news.

"Good place to learn reporting," my first editor said. "For most people, the newspaper obituary is the last thing ever printed about them. The obit you write will be clipped out and put into the family Bible. Make sure it's right." To be dispatched with an inaccurate obit was both a human and journalistic indignity.

I also check obituaries to see what they say about people's work. A few read like a résumé, with inflated litanies of professional achievement. Others do the reverse, skipping anything related to work. In effect, they say, "Look, this person had a life beyond work."

Such was the case with my friend Jack. He ran a small music store near my home back when I was lurching through adolescence and dreaming of a career as a musician. I often dropped in to buy sheet music, records (remember them?), or a bottle of trumpet valve oil. Or just to chat.

A kind and wise older man who had played in a lot of big bands, Jack offered tidbits of counsel that helped stabilize my stormy youth. His little store, his means of livelihood, was more than a place of commercial transactions. For me, it was an inviting place of warmth and affirmation.

Then I moved away. When I returned many years later, Jack's store was gone and he was dying. At his memorial service, I heard not a word about Jack's long career or the place where he had mentored me. As I listened, I wondered if I had stumbled into the wrong funeral. Where was the Jack I had known? It was as if he had never worked. Perhaps those who planned his memorial service didn't know his work was important. But it was important to me, at least.

Recently I heard echoes of Jack's memorial when someone declared, "I'm going to write my own obituary to make sure it says nothing about my business." That's a pity—not only because readers will be deprived of vital information, but also because he thinks there is little lasting value in the activity that has consumed most of his waking hours for four decades.

There was a time when gravestones told tales of those who lay beneath. Like this one from many centuries back: "Here lies Dion, a pious man; he lived 80 years and planted 4,000 trees."

"When I die," says William Rentschler, former chair of Medart Corporation, "I hope whoever delivers the eulogy will remember me as one who sought always to provide steady, decent, challenging jobs, which allowed good people to support their families, build and retain their self-esteem, and [quoting Teddy Roosevelt] 'work hard at work worth doing.' "

Here's a task to kick off the New Year: Why not write your own obituary? Ponder how you'd like to be remembered. Include the things most important to you. Let us peek into your soul. If you are bold, show it to some close friends. Does it ring true to them? If not, why not devote this year to becoming the person you want to be?

And don't forget to include your work.

If Jesus came to the office

Imagine Jesus dropping by your workplace. Would you have to grab for the Rolaids?

Here's what happened when Jesus visited Fred, owner of Acme Construction:

"Nice place, Fred. Looks efficient. Say, I really like the way you do trusses nowadays. Sure beats how we used to make them."

"Thanks, Lord. We try to keep up."

"So tell me, how are things going?"

"Uh, well, I have to admit my church work has lagged a bit. And I feel bad for declining that denominational board position. . . ."

"Fred."

"Yes?"

"Relax. This isn't a test."

"Right. I guess I'm a bit jumpy; I don't get a visit like this every day. Maybe I feel guilty for not doing more, but I don't have much energy left at the end of a day. It's all I can do to drag myself to choir practice on Thursdays. More evening meetings just don't make sense."

"I'm not wild about evening meetings myself."

"You aren't?"

"Nope. Actually, Fred, I want your best hours.

During the day. When you're fresh."

"But, but, that's when I'm working."

"Exactly. So let's start again. How does Acme compare with, say, the company down the street? How are you different?"

"Different?"

"Yeah. How do you define your mission? How are you using the gifts my Dad gave you?"

"Hmmm. Well, when the Christian high school needed a new addition, I put it up at cost. Didn't make a dime. And when that tornado went through the Midwest, I sent some of my people to help with reconstruction."

"That's great, Fred. But besides those extra things, what is special about your *daily* work? How do you do business differently? And I don't mean by printing little fish on your invoices."

"Frankly, Lord, just keeping my head above water takes most of my time. It's not that easy being in business these days—recession, unions, building codes. . . ."

"Hey, tell me about it. I used to swing a hammer myself. I built a lot of cabinets before I preached the Sermon on the Mount."

"Oh, yeah. The Sermon on the Mount. Suddenly I feel guilty again."

"Skip the guilt, Fred. I'm more interested in performance."

"Performance?"

"Yes. I'd like to know how you're modeling my

kingdom in your little corner of the business world. Right here. Right now."

"Uh, Lord, can we pick this up later? Senior management is meeting at ten to handle some marketing and personnel problems. While we're doing that, you can have donuts and coffee in the lunchroom, and maybe read the paper."

"Actually, Fred, your meeting sounds more interesting. Mind if I sit in?"

"You mean you'd join our meeting? I didn't know you cared about that sort of stuff."

"You'd be surprised, Fred."

Second-mile service

Martin Luther extolled faithful work: "God even milks the cow through you." He didn't say much about letter carriers, so let me try.

Peter Epp had spent nearly a year in a Soviet prison, long before we in the West ever heard the words *glasnost* or *perestroika*. He was tortured but never found out why.

When they finally released him, he was sent to a labor camp near the Arctic Circle. For a decade he worked in a uranium mine, cut off from family. It was a brutal life of toil and deprivation.

Stories like this are common among the Russian Mennonites who were finally permitted to emigrate in the late 1980s. But for us, this story is special.

Peter, you see, is family.

He is a relative I didn't know we had. My late grandfather had talked of kinfolk who hadn't made it out of Russia. When Stalin scattered what was left of the Mennonites, contact was broken.

Peter was one of those relatives. Thanks to the Gorbachev reforms, he had managed to emigrate to Germany.

Now, in his late 60s, he was here in Canada to meet his extended family.

What a wonderful visit it was! For a month he circulated among us. There were tears, laughter, stories, and rekindled memories as a frozen chapter of family history was thawed and brought to life.

His visit was made possible by some unknown civil servant who went to extra effort to do the job right. Maybe he was someone who believes in doing everything "as unto the Lord."

Peter Epp had been at a loss as to how to track down his missing family. When he settled in Germany, he wrote a letter to my maternal grandmother, not knowing she had passed away ten years earlier. He addressed it to "Margaret Epp, Steinbach USA."

Right town. Wrong country.

The USA is a big place. Steinbach isn't. It's a town of about 9,000 in southeastern Manitoba. Not many American postal clerks have ever heard of it. Who knows what head-scratching the letter caused when none of the fifty states had a Steinbach. Someone, however, must have cared enough to check another country. If they hadn't bothered, no one would have noticed.

Whatever they did, it worked. After two months the letter finally arrived in the right town, where the name Epp is well-known. Soon we were reconnected.

I'd heard of this kind of thing happening to celebrities, like the foreign letter sent years ago to "Billy Graham, Many Apples, Many Sodas." I didn't think it was still possible in this day of electronic sorting and dead-letter boxes.

So now we have a bigger family. An expanded circle of fellowship. A new store of precious memories.

We also have enduring gratitude for some anonymous friend in a postal station somewhere.

Someone who knows the meaning of second-mile service.

Daddy, would you write for *Playboy*?

When my sons were much younger, too young to know without asking, they posed an ethical dilemma to their journalist dad.

"Would you write an article for *Playboy* magazine if you had the chance?"

With four eyes upon me, I was quick to answer, "No, of course not."

"What if," one of them persisted, "you were out of work and we were broke and didn't have any food in the house, and *Playboy* offered you $5,000 to write an article?"

I was on the spot, but that was okay. Scott and Joel, both grade-schoolers, were taking some early steps into that great but often-gray world of applied Christian values. They wanted to know about situation ethics and the price of principle. And they weren't letting Papa wiggle off the hook with pious abstractions. They were adroitly lodging their questions in the real-life arena of faith and work.

They were asking, "What kinds of work fit those who follow Jesus?"

I'd faced the question before. A politician I interviewed early in my media career gravely urged me to quit the business as soon as possible. "Newspaper work is no place for a Christian," he said, likely reflecting his own unhappy experience with the press. I disagreed, believing then as now that my chosen profession is essentially good (though there are unhappy compromises, and I've made my share of them).

A pharmaceuticals executive is proud of his work with heart medications, but fears his company may venture into "home abortion" drugs. In that case he will be obliged, for reasons of conscience, to leave his job (and its six-figure salary).

A liquor distributor found himself attracted to Christ but stopped short of a commitment because then he would have to give up the career he had worked hard to build. He saw right away that his work would make a bad fit with Christian faith.

On the other hand, a prominent evangelical businessman sees no conflict between his faith and the pornographic magazines distributed by one of his subsidiaries. "It's just business," he argues.

In my Mennonite tradition, it is not uncommon to look with disfavor on jobs that contribute to the weapons industry.

What work won't we do? That is a good question for Christians.

The early church faced the same issue. History tells us that many new converts in the first and second century left the army when they accepted Jesus as Lord. Silversmiths changed occupations rather than make pagan idols. They were answering the same question: What work won't we do.

I leafed through several recent "faith and work" books and found some glaring omissions. Few of them examine the *kinds* of work that Christians do. Maybe they're afraid to explore the issue, because it is so contentious. Not all Christians agree on issues of liquor production, abortion, pollution, and military service.

Richard Foster makes a simple proposal in his book *Money, Sex and Power*: "As believers we affirm work that enhances human life and shun work that destroys human life." Well, it *sounds* simple, at least. Deciding what exactly is life-enhancing and life-destroying is more complex. He suggests prayer groups and "clearness meetings" to help believers find their place in the world of work.

Foster is right. The issue should be talked about in the discerning community. For many Christians, the issue is too big to handle alone.

What kind of work won't you do? Where do you draw the line between good work and bad? Who helps you draw that line and stand your ground?

February

Getting it together

Imagine a new Bible version that would clearly separate our Monday-to-Friday work from God's purposes. Some favorite passages would sound quite different.

Psalm 24 might begin: "The earth is the Lord's and everything in it *except the marketplace. . . ."*

Jesus' message in Matthew 5:16 could read: "Let your light shine before people, *but don't bother during business hours. . . ."*

That would seem strange. Yet many Christians do that when they put work and faith into separate compartments, as if God cares about one but not the other.

Christians don't do this deliberately. Most of us want to connect our faith and work. We don't go to work Monday morning and think, "Whew, I'm glad Sunday's over. Now I can pick up my life again." Nonetheless, that kind of thinking has sneaked up on us.

When it comes to missions, the division is even sharper. We're not accustomed to hearing work and mission in the same breath, especially if the work happens to be business. Professions like teaching and healthcare might border on mission, but what about business? That's like mixing broccoli and ice cream.

Some years ago I was asked to speak at a Christian business conference. "What's your topic?" a friend asked.

"Business and mission."

"Oh, so you're going to speak twice."

A mother was describing her grown children's vocational choices: "Our eldest went into business. The other one is serving the Lord."

I'm not addicted to work. Work wasn't one of those things I liked instantly, like chocolate. It was an acquired taste, like asparagus.

I received a lot of help acquiring this taste for work. As a youth I spent a lot of time hoeing onions on the family farm. During that drudgery, I made a startling discovery. I realized that work was going to be a significant part of my life.

Later I worked in the pizza business, and then I worked for daily newspapers and magazines. At each step my original insight was confirmed: Work was not something that was likely to go away.

I find that work takes up a lot of my time. It also forms a large part of my identity. I'm often defined by my job. When I meet someone new, it usually doesn't take long before the question comes up, "And what do you *do*?"

Work forms a large part of my waking hours. It also helps define who I am. Therefore, I want to make it count for something beyond a paycheck.

I am a follower of Christ. So it only makes sense that this part of my life, which starts Monday morning and occupies most of my energy for the next five days, should be part of the life of discipleship.

William Diehl has said that if we don't make the effort to connect our faith and our work, we trivialize our faith: "Something that has no relevance to those places where we spend most of our time cannot, after all, be very important."

Therefore, if my Christian faith is important, then it's important enough to apply to all of life.

That includes the marketplace.

The Bible at your desk

What does the Bible say about your job?

Some people look to the Bible for pithy sayings that might have a business application: "Anyone unwilling to work should not eat" (2 Thess. 3:10, NRSV). Or they use some of the stories of Jesus, like the parable of the talents, which teaches wise stewardship. Neither of these, however, gets to the heart of the gospel message.

A more extreme level calls for taking on the attitude of Christ (Phil. 2:4-9, NIV).

My friend John Eby uses a baking analogy to illustrate degrees of integration:

• The most basic level, superficial piety, is like putting frosting on a cake: you add a layer of sweetness, but beneath it all you still have the same cake.

• Another level is like chocolate chips in a cookie: they are part of the cookie, yet distinctly separate and isolated.

• A third level is like the yeast in bread: it permeates the dough and actually transforms its essence and behavior.

That third level intrigues me. I've wondered, How could we act as yeast in our places of work?

To be yeast might mean asking probing questions

about our work. What public good will my work accomplish today? Is my work an important part of God's economy? Is the world a better place because of the work I do?

Does our work contribute to the kind of world God intends, where deserts become fertile fields, where parched lands become glad, where waste spaces are comforted, as the Old Testament prophets say?

How can we match our daily behavior, profits, and ethics to God's plan for humanity? Can we become servants of society by producing goods and services that enhance life rather than harm it?

If you are a manager or business owner, how can you be yeast? It may mean serving our employees and recognizing them as stakeholders and not merely as a means of production. It means placing human value above economic value.

It means asking whether our ever-increasing technology is life-enhancing or life-destroying.

It means asking some serious questions about competition, not only between corporate competitors but also between co-workers.

It means dealing with the kinds of brokenness we run across in the workplace. It means dealing redemptively with failure, whether a business bankruptcy or a failed employee.

It means running a risk for the sake of an ideal. Honesty at all costs is risky. Going the second mile with a problem employee is risky.

I'm going to spend this week examining what my workplace would be like if my presence became like yeast. Care to join me?

God's double agents

Scott, my oldest son, asked a good question in church one day and I became annoyed. Not with him, but with a Bible college professor to whom the question was addressed.

At the time, Scott was finishing an undergraduate degree in science. He spent that summer doing research on a disease I can't pronounce and hope never to get. He went on to do graduate studies in biochemistry.

Scott is also theologically literate, and when he asks a question it's usually a dilly. The Bible college professor, apparently impressed, took him aside afterward and suggested Scott consider "the ministry." That's when I took umbrage.

"Maybe Scott *is* considering the ministry," I retorted. "Maybe biochemistry *is* a field of ministry."

I kept going. "Do we really need more professional ministers in our denomination? Maybe what we need are scientists who want to do God's will."

The professor had struck a nerve. I often encounter the view that serious, committed Christians should go into full-time paid ministry, while "secular" jobs are for the rest of us second-class citizens.

Can't a job be a part of ministry? We all know

that pastors have a ministry and missionaries have a ministry. But do editors have ministries? How about teachers, farmers, accountants, plumbers, librarians, truck drivers? Whatever happened to "the priesthood of all believers"?

The marketplace can be a unique launchpad for mission. People who work there have special access to the world that professional ministers don't have. They have something special to contribute to the kingdom of God, and it's not just money. There are some things they can do that others can't. Someone has said that Christians in the marketplace are like God's double agents—they have a foot in the church and a foot in the world.

When we go to work, we carry the kingdom of God along with us. One of our tasks is to transform our little corner of the world into an outpost of that kingdom.

Graham Tucker, an Anglican minister who founded a workplace chaplaincy in Toronto's financial district, urges Christian workers to conjure up a picture of what the kingdom of God is like. Then, he says, imagine the kingdom of God (the reign of Christ) in your place of work—in your office, your classroom, your factory, or your farm.

What would your workplace be like if it were a little corner of the kingdom, a place where Christ reigned? Try to visualize how things would be. How would people treat each other? How would staff treat clients or customers? What kinds of goods and services might you produce . . . or not produce? How would you treat the competition? How would you treat that irritating co-worker who makes life miserable for you?

God calls us to be agents of the kingdom in everything we do. Seeing our work as part of God's mission might just transform how we look at Monday morning.

Think of that when you go to work tomorrow. Think of yourself as God's double agent. Think of yourself as embarking on a ministry, a ministry to which God has called you, a ministry for which you have special skills.

I'll bet it'll put a spring in your step.

Thawing out
frozen assets

It must be an unusual church. Above every door leading outward is a sign saying Servant's Entrance. The signs are on the inside, precisely where most buildings have signs saying Exit.

William Diehl mentions this church in his book *Thank God, It's Monday*. The signs remind people that the real ministry of the church is not "in here" but "out there" in society.

Most Christians know that. But still we often think of ministry as what goes on within the walls of the meetinghouse.

In many churches, "lay ministry" means letting ordinary folk help out with programs, lead worship, or preach once in a while. That's not bad, but it's not the whole story. Congregations aren't the entire kingdom.

Paul Stevens, in his book *Liberating the Laity*, describes two kinds of lay ministers, one in the world and one in the church. These are also called Type A and Type B, or outward and inward laypersons.

Those of Type A (outward) are involved in particular careers or professions and see their focus as the "church in dispersion." Type B (inward) persons are essentially volunteer clergy who are more concerned about the gathered church.

Outward types may have less to do with midweek or Sunday services. They see their mission as pressing the kingdom upon their workplace activities. Inward types are likely to emphasize congregational structures, programs, and committees.

Much lay ministry training leans inward: how to teach Sunday school or lead a small-group Bible study. These are fine, but Stevens calls them "come structures"—the message they communicate is "come and hear" or "come and see." Also needed are "go structures" that send Christians out into the world.

This world includes our places of work, where we spend so much of our time anyway. That's where most of us actually confront "the powers" (competition, conflict, and injustice, to name a few). That's where we really exercise our spiritual muscles.

Stevens suggests that if we always focus inward on a congregational or even denominational program, large resources are paralyzed, as if suspended in a block of ice. These are "the frozen assets of the church."

How do we thaw these resources? One way is to see our own workweek as a ministry to which God has called us, and then help our congregations do the same. This will not dilute the church's ministry by shifting attention away from the congregation. Instead, it will greatly expand our ministry and help activate nonperforming assets.

Spring is just around the corner. The earth is ready to awake from slumber. A great thaw is coming.

Will it also reach the church?

March

With friends
like these . . .

I was aghast to read in the morning paper that my friend Russell had been charged with embezzlement. Later that day we met over coffee.

Russell's life had collapsed almost overnight. He'd lost his prestigious job and vacated his upscale house on scenic country acreage. He'd moved into a rented apartment. A friend had given him a part-time job while he awaits trial. Russell hoped he could salt away a few dollars for his wife because he expects to spend some time getting, as he puts it, "free room and board from the government."

Russell was groping for silver linings. Aside from experiencing the overwhelming disgrace, he says he feels an almost perverse sense of relief. For five years he was on a career treadmill. Work opportunities soared, as did his appetite for the "good life." The higher he rose in the professional ranks, the more lifestyle adjustments he made to support his image.

"I have to slow down," he told himself over and over again. But like a compulsive drinker or gambler, he could not control the hunger for more. Finally he became so highly leveraged that in a cash-flow pinch, he "borrowed" someone else's assets to cover a shortfall. Then he dipped into another account to pay back the first one. And so on.

"Maybe I got caught just in time," he mused.

As he described his plight it dawned on me that I hadn't been a good friend to Russell. I should have heeded the signals. I should have mentioned something when I noticed him becoming consumed by his work, when he stopped coming to some of the church events we used to attend together.

If I'd been more sensitive, I might have recognized the signs of stress in his life: mood swings and a growing tendency to isolate himself. I even might have confronted him on his increasingly overheated lifestyle and upscale tastes. That's hard to do without sounding judgmental.

We live in a "mind your own business" society. We don't want people to stick their noses into our personal affairs. How would I like to be confronted on how I am pursuing my career goals? After all, my work is my ministry, so don't tell me I'm too ambitious. Yet even ministers need a seasoned voice of friendship when workplace zeal nears fever pitch.

Someone needs to tell us, as Jethro told his son-in-law Moses, "What you are doing is not good. You will surely wear yourself out . . ." (Exod. 18:17, NRSV). The problem was overwork. Moses was heading for burnout because he didn't know how to delegate authority. Jethro took him aside and gave him one of Scripture's first lessons in management.

That kind of intervention may be seen as a threat to privacy. But isn't that an essential part of Christian mutual support?

"The Lord looked and was . . . appalled that there was no one to intervene . . ." (Isa. 59:15-16, NIV).

When it came to Russell, I didn't intervene. If I had, if someone had, maybe he wouldn't be wallowing in humiliation, his life in tatters, waiting to find out how long he is going to be a guest of the government.

Lighten up

A police officer was called to an apartment block to respond to a domestic dispute. As he approached the building, he heard yelling and the sound of shattering glass. He looked up to see a television set fly out of a second-floor window and crash to the ground below. The officer raced up the stairs and rang the doorbell.

"Who's there?" demanded an angry voice inside.

"Television repair," the officer deadpanned.

There was silence for a few seconds, and finally the door was opened by a man with a sheepish grin.

The quick-thinking officer had helped to defuse a serious situation. It was something he'd learned in a "humor course" the police department had arranged.

Humor has always been an informal staple of workplace survival. It's gaining new respectability as studies show its value in reducing stress, creating a positive work climate, and even increasing productivity.

People who laugh a lot work better and faster. In one study, 84 percent of executives and personnel directors reported that employees with a sense of humor did better work. Some businesses even hire humor consultants to boost employee motivation, communication, and creativity.

People in a good mood organize data better, are more creative in word association, and do better with tasks involving memory. Humor also improves decision-making and negotiating abilities. Those who have fun at work are also more satisfied with their jobs, better able to meet the demands of the job, and less likely to be absent or late.

Some scientists say laughter and playful behavior can trigger beneficial chemical and physiological changes in the body. Laughter reduces worker stress and boosts productivity because it increases blood circulation, feeds oxygen to the brain, and pumps out hormones that aid alertness. It also has been found to release the body's natural pain-killing endorphins and enhance the immune system.

Humor is one of the tools Christians can use to improve life in the workplace. We Christians are naturally happy people, so why not show it at work? Does it seem frivolous to use humor as an aid to work and spirituality?

"A cheerful heart is good medicine, but a crushed spirit dries up the bones," says Proverbs 17:22 (NIV). "Do not look dismal," Jesus says in Matthew 6:16 (NRSV). He spoke these words to people who were fasting, but there also is a message for those engaged in less-serious endeavors, like work.

In his book *The Humor of Christ*, Quaker author Elton Trueblood suggests that Jesus employed humor to make some of his most significant points. One who would talk about straining at gnats or squeezing a camel through a needle's eye was not a person without a sense of humor.

A leading hindrance to workplace spirituality is hostility and aggression. What better way to play the role of Christian peacemaker than by using humor to break down barriers and open channels of communication!

Small tensions often vaporize in the presence of humor. John Gerstner tells of the time he filled up at a highway truck stop. He and another customer arrived at the cashier's stall at the same time. Who goes first at a time like that, especially if you're both in a hurry? The cashier handled it well. In a deadpan voice she asked, "Which of you has the gas?"

After that, neither motorist minded who went first.

Little white anecdotes

Some years ago a prominent television preacher was caught making untrue and exaggerated claims about what he had said during an audience with the U.S. president. Confronted with the discrepancies, he dismissed them as "little white anecdotes."

Most of us can relate to that. I'm sure we've all stretched the truth to get out of a tight spot. "I'll get right on it." "I liked your sermon." "The check's in the mail."

When you get right down to it, these "little white anecdotes" are lies.

To lie is to make an untrue statement or create a false and misleading impression. Scripture gives clear signals as to what God thinks about lying. "Lying lips are an abomination unto the Lord," says Proverbs 12:22.

Life in the marketplace offers countless occasions to lie. Personnel specialists say a phenomenal percentage of job-seekers lie on their résumés. Many people lie when giving references. It's not always easy to be candid when giving a referral for a friend, or for an employee you're secretly glad to see leaving.

If you're a CEO, how honest are you if an employee asks how the business is doing? If the out-look is gloomy, telling the truth may sour the employee's mood and performance.

How honest should you be in dealing with clients? It's tough to admit that the competition might be able to match your quality and price.

Many years ago I wanted to sell my house in Kansas because I was moving across the country. My house had a leaky basement. After a serious rain, half the basement would be covered with an inch of water. I wondered how honest I'd be with prospective buyers. What would I say if they asked me point-blank about the basement?

When the agent called to say some people would come by next morning to look at the house, my hands got sweaty. The hour of candor loomed.

Apparently, God didn't think I was up to the challenge. That night there was a terrific rainstorm. By morning my basement was soaked. No explanations were necessary. We did need rubber boots, though.

From a purely practical standpoint, being honest usually pays off in the long run. It produces a good reputation and repeat business.

It's also much easier. "I always tell the truth," said one businessman. "That way I don't have to bother remembering what I've said." Another person agrees: "It's easy to tell a lie, but hard to tell only one. The first lie must be thatched with another, and another, and another, or it will rain through."

Keeping track of all the effects of a lie is just too much work.

Christians have better reasons for telling the truth. Truth-telling is part of what it means to be a redeemed community.

Even small lies, the "little white anecdotes" of daily life, eventually add up, like calories. It's the little grains of sand that can wear down the gears.

When ethical structures crumble, it's because they've been weakened piece by piece. Moral foundations are built the same way. Brick by brick. By you and by me. In the small places of life.

Rules of the game

Fred and I used to love playing Monopoly. In the midst of a game, you'd never know we were buddies. Normally Fred was kind and generous, but land on his Boardwalk with a hotel, and he'd demand every last dollar of rent. A look of perverse glee would cross his usually benign face as he looked forward to squeezing me dry.

"Being nice" was not part of the game. The only way to play was to be hard-nosed and greedy. The ultimate goal was to bankrupt the other player. We played by rules we'd never use in real life.

However, it didn't matter because we had agreed that this was the way to play. Part of the fun was to suspend customary niceties for the duration of the game.

Monopoly came to mind when I ran across an article from the *Harvard Business Review* of thirty years ago. Albert Z. Carr asked, "Is Business Bluffing Ethical?" The essay has become a classic in ethics debates.

Carr likened business to a game of poker in which bluffing is a key tactic. Since all players expect you to do it, it's not really wrong. "No one expects poker to be played on the ethical principles preached in churches," he wrote. "In poker, it is right and proper to bluff a friend out of the rewards of being dealt a good hand."

I think most Christian businesspeople would disagree with Carr. "Bluff" is just a polite term for "deceive," and Scripture insists that God has little patience with deceit. We also know that deceit doesn't pay over the long haul.

However, the point of Carr's provocative article was not so much whether deceit is right or wrong, or whether being honest is good or bad for business. The issue was whether we use a different set of rules in business than we do in everyday life. According to Carr, the virtues of the church don't apply because business is a game where normal rules of life are set aside.

That would be easier to accept if business were in fact only a game. But it's not. In Monopoly, we fold up the game afterward, pack up Boardwalk and the hotels, and put it all on a shelf for the next rainy day.

It's not that way in business. The economic marketplace embraces everyone, not just a select few who can choose whether or not they want to play. A lot of people are affected by decisions we make behind the desk. The families of our employees have a stake in our corporate decisions but don't really have the power to decide what kinds of rules will be used. An entire community can suffer for years if we dump toxins into the local water supply.

The larger issue is whether the gospel has anything at all to do with the way we conduct ourselves during the week. For Christians, the answer is obvious. Few indictments are as damaging as the charge that our behavior does not match our beliefs.

We are more than Sunday Christians. The good news of the gospel penetrates all areas of our lives, not only some convenient compartments. The authenticity of our faith is tested less on Sunday morning than during a certain forty hours of the week.

Hans Denck, a sixteenth-century reformer, said it best: "No one can truly know Christ without following him in daily life."

April

Kicking the bag

"When Ty Cobb reached first base, he had a nervous habit of kicking the bag. Not till he retired from the game did the secret come out. By kicking the bag hard enough, Cobb could move it a full two inches closer to second base. He figured that this improved his chances for a steal or for reaching second base safely on a hit."

The television preacher who told this story didn't disapprove of Cobb's ploy, though it was actually a form of cheating. In fact, the preacher thought it showed the spirit of a true competitor. He gave an implied message to young people in sports, business, and other pursuits: "Use any tricks you can to get an edge over someone else."

You don't have to look far to see that many others feel the same way. A business manual for those bounding upward suggests various tricks young executives can use to impress the boss. Here are two examples:

• Take your briefcase home from work every day, even if it's empty. People will think you're working after hours.

• If a superior wants to get together the next day, be quick to suggest an early start, like seven a.m.

This gives the impression that you always start work early.

Thus the manual implies that deceptions will give you a competitive edge over someone else.

Such subtle examples revive old images of business as sneaky and grasping. For a time, such negative stereotypes had faded as business sought a more caring and generous face. The popularity of excellent books like *Servant Leadership* by Robert Greenleaf has nourished a feeling that maybe kingdom ethics are becoming fashionable in the marketplace.

That is wishful thinking. Steely self-interest still ranks high on many business report cards, and may rank even higher in the future. Canadian business columnist Peter C. Newman contends that many business schools are "transforming would-be yuppies" into hard-edged, emotionless "masters of the bottom line."

Not untypical, he says, is a commerce graduate who twisted a classic slogan: "It's not how you play. It's whether you win the game."

Writer Ned Dewey appraises the new breed of Ivy League MBAs: "These kids are smart. But I'd as soon take a python to bed as hire one. He'd suck my brains, memorize my Rolodex, and use my telephone to find some other guy who'd pay him twice the money."

Tough talk, perhaps overstated. But it gives pause to those who thought business had shed its dark image. Let's not kid ourselves. There's still a lot of hardball being played out there.

I have two suggestions. First, let's give whole-hearted support to our Christian colleges' efforts to teach biblical values and ethics to future business leaders. They're striving to invest their graduates with a Christian understanding of the bottom line.

Second, let's review our own corporate behavior and check what kind of models we're being. Any time we kick the bag for a two-inch advantage or mislead someone for personal benefit, we teach others that greed, deception, and hard-core pragmatism are necessary for professional life.

The world still needs faithful people who will model the kingdom way in the marketplace.

Waddling down unfriendly aisles

The suburban shopping mall seemed to stretch on endlessly, lined on each side by dozens of stores with bright lights and colorful fronts that dazzled the eyes. I needed some new clothes and thought this magnificent array of outlets could meet my need.

The clerk in the first store clucked disapprovingly as I maneuvered my bulk through narrow aisles stacked high with pants, shirts, sweaters, and vests. "I'm afraid," she breathed in hushed tones, "we have nothing in your size. Biggest we go is 40-inch waist."

In the next store, I fared worse. The head clerk glanced up from his order book, sized me up as a 46, and flashed me a frosty stare that said, "What do you think *you're* doing here?"

Two doors down looked more promising, or at least friendly. But when I got inside, the attendants avoided me, busying themselves with hangers and displays. They wouldn't even speak to me. I think I heard one mutter, "Why doesn't he try Western Tent and Awning?"

It was bad enough being portly. But the icy glares amid row after row of size 34 and 36 pants and size

17 shirts (tapered, naturally) made me feel like an alien in a hostile land, a leper among the healthy.

Wallowing in dejection, I left. The brightly lit plastic supermall had nothing for me, not even civility.

Then, miles away, I discovered it by accident. There, tucked behind a gas station and a Kwik-Trip, peeked the sign: Acme Big and Tall, We Fit 'Em All.

Skeptical, I sucked in as much of my paunch as I could and strode stiffly inside. What a shock! I found friendly clerks anxious to meet the needs of the most downtrodden porker. And clothes—all shapes and sizes of them, far bigger than I needed. Sixty-inch belts, triple-X shirts, size 15 double-width shoes.

The owner, it turned out, had once been too big to shop at "normal" stores. After slimming down, he decided to open a store catering to those who had once been in his shoes.

It felt good to be outfitted anew. It felt even better to be accepted by a warm clerk who kindly tolerated my flaws. "We get 'em much bigger than you," she assured me.

As I left, feeling affirmed and presenting a picture of sartorial splendor, I wondered if our churches are ever like the clothing stores I had encountered.

Are they sometimes like the snobbish shops in the mall, catering to the beautiful, the sleek and the slender, and coolly avoiding those who are so far from perfection?

Or are they more like the Big and Tall, welcoming the odd-shaped, the ungainly, and others who don't fit society's image of acceptability?

A church isn't a store. But sometimes a store can be like a church.

Both can make the "odd ones" feel welcome and accepted.

Both have something that will meet their need.

Shy about God?

The CEO and his company had been glowingly featured in a top business magazine. Yet he was unhappy. The writer had completely ignored the spiritual side of his business.

That's too bad. If faith was important to the man's operation, it was poor journalism to exclude it. But then the media often falls short in religious matters.

The other day I ran across the problem in reverse: a journalist for a secular periodical who complained that Christians in business don't talk enough about their faith.

"The absence of God is never more striking than in reading business magazines," says the editor of *Across the Board*, published by The Conference Board. The typical CEO profile pays wearisome attention to a subject's heroes, hobbies, pets, politics, and investments. But the profile makes little mention of faith other than perhaps a passing reference to someone being active in a local church.

Nine out of ten North Americans say they believe in God. "Yet in matters of business, God is most noticeable by his absence."

Don't blame this on sloppy journalism, however.

Editor Al Vogl insists the problem lies elsewhere: "CEOs and other business executives are shy about professing their beliefs in God when the talk is about business." They hide their light under a bushel.

He recounts his interview with a prominent CEO known as a grand old man of business ethics. During a lengthy discussion of ethics in leadership, the CEO never once mentioned God. He happens, by the way, to be an evangelical Christian.

I can relate to that. In an earlier life, I covered business for a daily newspaper. Rarely would businessfolk (many of whom I knew were Christians) bring up their faith unless coaxed.

Why this Trappist vow of silence? Here are some possible reasons:

• Maybe we just don't want to seem boastful or proud. We don't want to sound like self-righteous Christians who pretend to have a corner on God's favor.

• We're afraid the reporter won't care or understand. It's scary to see a reporter's eyes glaze over.

• We're worried that our "walk" doesn't match our talk. If a reporter finds ethical lapses (and we all have them, at least I do), we'll be seen as hypocrites.

• We don't want other businessfolk to think we're pushovers: "She won't take us to court; she's a Christian."

• We want to fit in. In *The Culture of Disbelief,*

Stephen Carter tells of a man who was advised by a headhunter to play down his involvement with a church-related social welfare organization. The headhunter thought he would be less marketable if he came across as a religious fanatic.

• We're tired of "business testimonies" that seem trite. After all, do we really believe our success is due to God's blessing when the CEO in the next pew has just gone bankrupt? The dissonance is troubling. Until we sort it out, we'd just as soon keep still.

• Some of us are not yet convinced that *our work is really a ministry.* Our churches don't always help on this matter, which doesn't exactly boost our self-confidence.

When God is clearly at the heart of our workday week, we'll be more at ease in showing our colors.

Which type is your company?

How many different ways are there to be socially responsible in business? One of my favorite Christian newsletters suggests that there are three basic types.

1. The corporation as philanthropist. These folks make money and use it to support good causes. They meet the biblical injunction to "honor the Lord with your wealth, with the firstfruits of all your crops" (Prov. 3:9, NIV). Many vital ministries and social services would find it hard to function if it weren't for the generosity of companies like these. Would that there were more of them!

A problem arises, however, when companies think their generosity lets them off the moral hook for other behavior. I heard one prominent manufacturer say, "Don't talk to me about greed. Leave me alone to run my company. The more money I make, the more I can give to missions."

Another extreme example is a tobacco company that has become well-known for pouring huge amounts of money into the arts. Is a company like that really trying to improve the world, or just to silence its critics? When New York City was considering a strict antismoking measure, the company called on its friends in the arts community to lobby against it.

2. *The corporation as provider of socially desirable products or services.* This type of company makes a point of connecting its output with certain ideals, such as a bank that invests in decaying communities, or a manufacturer that produces environmentally safe products. Conversely, some companies avoid certain kinds of business involvements for ethical reasons. Some investors screen out certain stocks from their portfolios (like companies that produce tobacco, alcohol, weapons, or questionable magazines).

Critics say such ideals are fine, as long as the company stays solvent. But would it still be socially responsible to go broke producing a natural deodorant if it meant jeopardizing the livelihood of the workforce? What's more important in the grand scheme of things—a socially responsible product, or a stable bottom line that maintains jobs and security in the community?

3. *The corporation as enlightened employer.* This company discharges its social responsibility by being especially good to its employees and making the workplace into a kind of community. Such a company has a strong employee assistance program (EAP), on-site family care center, a fitness facility, and literacy programs.

When refugees moved into the community, the company hired a number of them and organized a program to teach them English as a second language. It gives employees a piece of the action, not only through profit sharing and employee stock ownership, but also through open access to corporate information.

Fundraisers aren't so sure they like this kind of company. When an agency representative visited one such CEO to solicit support, the CEO said, "Why should I give you a check? I can do more good with our profits by reinvesting them in the company."

Do these three types cover the field? Are there others? Do you know of companies that fit all three categories?

Where would you like to fit in?

May

Death and revenue enhancement

My first newspaper job was writing obituaries. The editor gave me a fast lesson in euphemisms.

"Don't write 'passed away' or 'went to a heavenly reward.' Around here we say 'died.' Calling it something else doesn't lessen anyone's grief and just takes up extra space."

Today he'd have more terms to ban, like "negative patient care outcome." Society seems fond of euphemisms and doublespeak.

A euphemism is an agreeable term we substitute for one that may offend or sound unpleasant. It's a way to avoid stating the truth, like calling vandalism "souvenir hunting." The hope is that a pleasant term will make the news less painful.

It doesn't work.

If my wife examines the checkbook and says, "We have a negative cash flow," I don't feel any happier than if she'd said, "We're broke."

If my boss calls me into his office and says, "I'm going to free up your future," I won't feel much better than if he'd said, "You're fired."

Doublespeak dodges or obscures meaning. It puts truth a step or two farther away. The apostle Paul might have called it clanging brass.

We're accustomed to hearing doublespeak from academics and bureaucrats.

When an air force missile flew out of control, it didn't really crash. It simply "impacted with the ground prematurely."

In 1964 the U.S. State Department said it would no longer use the word "killing" in reporting the status of human rights around the world. Instead, it would refer to "unlawful or arbitrary deprivation of life."

Politicians who promised not to raise taxes can institute "revenue enhancement." (Nothing in life is certain except negative patient care outcome and revenue enhancement.) Lies are commonly called "misspeaking."

A newspaper identified a man sleeping in a skid-row doorway as "a non-goal-oriented member of society."

A person who jumped off a tall building had the misfortune of suffering "sudden deceleration trauma." The body was taken to a mortician whose work was described as "the final step in the health care delivery system."

Perhaps the last place to expect doublespeak is in business, known for no-nonsense clarity and precision. Alas, we find it even there.

If you were put out of work when an automaker closed an east-coast assembly plant, you could take comfort in knowing that it was merely a "volume-related production schedule adjustment." See how many groceries that buys!

If you were one of 5,000 workers another automaker laid off in Wisconsin, you could tell your spouse, "Great news, dear, the company initiated a career alternative enhancement program today, and I'm part of it."

The nuclear energy industry, meanwhile, has a reassuring new term for radiation leaks: "migration." And a plant explosion isn't an explosion at all but a "rapid release of energy." Whew, that's a relief!

The doublespeak award, however, goes to the stockbroker who stubbornly asserted that the stock market crash of a few years ago was nothing more than a "fourth quarter equity retreat."

How far we have strayed, with our verbal pollution, from the message of him who taught us to let our yes be yes, and let our no be no!

In praise of small steps

Some friends returned from an overseas church agency assignment. They were downcast because they had not achieved more. There was so much hunger and poverty to wrack the soul. Despite their diligence and commitment, they could do so little. In a vast sea of need, they felt like bobbing corks.

That's not uncommon among those who have seen massive human suffering. It's part of our well-meaning (or arrogant?) Western nature to want to "do something" to remedy problems. It is another part of this nature to want to see quick results. "Let's help the poor, and let's do it by Tuesday after-noon."

Seasoned mission and development workers know that change seldom comes promptly or on schedule. People who want to share their skills and resources with the world's poor need to plug in for the long haul.

Businesspeople have an image of being impatient types who want quick results. No doubt some are, particularly speculators who want to make a fast buck. But society's real producers have perseverance in large measure.

The development of quality, service, market

share, employee loyalty, brand recognition, and new products takes patience and persistence. Businesspeople have a healthy understanding of small increments in the larger scheme of success.

That is why they have a role to play in helping solve huge social problems requiring long-range strategy, like global poverty, hunger, and economic disparity. Though they are concerned about effectiveness, they know the value of small steps.

Few huge evils have been foisted on humankind en masse. They develop over time, piece by piece and layer by layer. Tiny evils add up to enormities.

We undo them in similar fashion: not by amassing forces and zapping the world with a monolithic "good," but by strategically adding up many successive acts of faithful discipleship.

Benjamin Franklin said, "Little strokes fell great oaks." Lucretius said, "Falling drops at last will wear the stone." A bee, we are told, must visit 56,000 clover heads for a pound of honey.

Jesus talked about mustard seeds, and about little doses of salt and light.

A Canadian businessman once asked the chairman of Toyota how the Japanese had managed to capture such a hefty share of North America's market for consumer goods.

"There is no secret," the man replied through interpreters. "The whole of Japan has a strategy, a national strategy of commitment to quality."

How, the Canadian wanted to know, did they

teach more than a hundred million people about quality?

The chairman replied, "One by one."

Rush to judgment

A famous retailer was known for making snappy judgments over dinner. If a prospective employee reached for the saltshaker before tasting the food, the interview was over. The executive didn't want to hire a creature of hidebound habit.

The other day a business magazine reported how a lodging chain winnowed hundreds of applicants for jobs in a new hotel. While the applicants waited to be interviewed, company staff studied their every move. Those who didn't smile at least four times while standing in line were automatically rejected.

Many of us, at least occasionally, judge people on appearance. We prejudge, making an evaluation without sufficient information. Another word for it is prejudice.

The businessfolk cited above must be better than I at making quick judgments based on scant data. I've often been wrong when I've tried to size people up by appearances. A company executive for whom I once worked was seriously unimpressive at first sight; his ties were always the wrong width, and he wore his lunch on his lapels. Yet he turned out to be one of the most competent bosses I've ever had.

Conversely, a colleague in the advertising department cast a terrific impression with his coiffed hair and dapper duds. Too bad he couldn't sell ads.

One of the hard lessons I learned early in journalism was not to judge a situation before the facts were in. A federal election had been called, and my newspaper sent me to cover the nominating meeting of one of the national political parties.

As I approached the auditorium, I was taken in by the fancy posters for three candidates who wanted to be their party's standard bearer. Inside, the hall was a circus of colorful placards for the three candidates—two of them lawyers and one a sociology professor.

I listened to the three candidates and took plenty of notes. They were impressive. Their words flowed like honey. They wore handsome suits and fashionable haircuts. After the third one sat down, there was a commotion at the back of the hall. A little man elbowed his way to the platform. He was a late entry in the race and wasn't even on the printed list of candidates.

His suit was wrinkled. He wasn't polished like the others. He didn't speak well. His words didn't flow in smooth phrases.

I was so sure he wasn't a serious candidate that I didn't even take notes. That was a mistake.

You already know who won.

I had really blown it. My story was slated for the next day's front page, and I hadn't taken any notes!

However, the rumpled little candidate bailed me

out. He graciously lent me the manuscript of his speech so I could take it back to the office and play catch-up. Despite my foolishness, I managed to assemble a story that made it onto page one. The candidate wound up winning the election to become the next Member of Parliament for that region.

I learned something that I should have learned from reading the book of James: "Suppose a man comes into your meeting wearing a gold ring and fine clothes, and a poor man in shabby clothes also comes in. If you show special attention to the man wearing fine clothes, . . . have you not . . . become judges with evil thoughts?" (2:2-4, NIV).

A good lesson for journalists.

And for those in business.

Get a whiff of this

The publisher shook his head. No, he didn't think the book-buying public was eagerly awaiting a scratch-and-sniff Bible.

I thought the idea had been brilliant—odor enhancements to bring old Bible stories to life.

For example, at the story of Noah's ark, you'd scratch the margin, and the aroma of camels and elephants would waft up from the page. Scratch beside Matthew 6 and detect lilies of the field. Turn over a few pages and smell the fish that fed five thousand.

I got the idea from a spice company whose annual report smells like seasonings. One year it smelled like gingerbread. Another year it was vanilla. Then nutmeg.

Although I've given up on a scratch-and-sniff Bible, I still think our sense of smell deserves more attention.

Smell is one of our most powerful senses. It has a terrific sense of history. A mere whiff of something can trigger a memory from childhood.

Among my favorites are the ocean, lilacs in June, freshly cut clover, a newly opened package of coffee, bedsheets dried in the sunshine, and believe it or not, a stable of horses.

The nose can warn of danger, like leaking gas in your house. It can tell you that milk is sour or meat has gone bad.

It can also give comfort, like the fragrance of a warm wet washcloth. Or tell you that the neighbors have fired up their barbecue.

Smells play a role in the world of work and business.

A real estate agent says the bouquet of baking bread can help sell a house.

Scientists have found a link between scents and workplace performance. Lavender and jasmine relax employees and cut stress. Lemon, meanwhile, stimulates. In some tests, workers made considerably fewer keypunching errors when these scents were pumped into the air.

The German poet Schiller reportedly kept spoiled apples handy for inspiration. A good sniff would sometimes dislodge the right word or phrase. This has never worked for me.

At one time a keen sniffer was regarded as a sign of spirituality. This was because smell deals with the unseen, the unfathomable, and other things associated with mystics. Smell has a mysterious power. There's no stopping it, no getting away from it. It invades every nook and cranny of a room. It can see around corners.

Scripture speaks of burnt sacrifices presenting a "pleasing odor" to God (Gen. 8:21, NRSV). Elsewhere we read of the stench of bad worship.

One of the first gifts to the Christ child was incense. Mary became the patron saint of perfume makers for anointing Christ's feet with precious ointment. Paul spoke of the fragrance that comes from knowing Christ (2 Cor. 2:14-16).

Bernard of Clairvaux likened the teachings of Christ to the aroma of flowers in full bloom. They utterly pervade our lives and exert their soothing influence in all directions.

My church tradition doesn't do much with smells. We don't use incense in worship, though some come to church doused with cologne. There seems to be a feeling that sight and sound are all we need to worship God.

I'd vote for including smell. The symbolic value alone would be helpful.

Think of it this way: Just as odor rises to fill every corner of a room, the Christian faith invades all of life, not just certain parts. Our Christian essence accompanies us everywhere.

Especially to work.

The business of theology

Sometimes I wonder who gets a worse bum rap, businesspeople or theologians.

Businesspeople often complain about being misunderstood, falsely accused, and unfairly stereotyped.

Theologians, I think, don't complain as much, but they could. They're often regarded as dry, monkish types who hunch over a desk in a remote tower, developing equally remote and towering philosophical thoughts about God.

Maybe businesspeople and theologians should get together and compare notes.

The other day a speaker said God doesn't care about theology and doctrine, but cares instead about behavior. That startled some of the assembled businessfolk. It sounded like heresy. But they warmed up in a hurry as they sensed good ammo for the next time a theologue throws some Hebrew or Harnack at them.

My Mennonite tradition sometimes has been cool to theology. The early Anabaptists regarded it as a hindrance to real Christian devotion. They feared that "simple pious love for Christ might be depraved and sterilized by theological speculation," says *The Mennonite Encyclopedia*. Besides, wasn't it the learned theologians of the sixteenth century who had persecuted us in the first place?

Theology isn't all that complicated. Literally, it is *logos* about *theos*, or thought and speech about God. One theologian defines his task simply as reflection about God and God's intervention in human affairs, "reflection on the Christian witness to determine its meaning and truth." This is surely the job of all Christians, including those who toil in the daily marketplace.

Another theologian defines the task as discovering how "human activity should be molded once it has been touched by [divine] intervention." Yet another sees theology as "a way of viewing things from a God point of view." Who of us would not want to be accused of that? Imagine running a business "from a God point of view."

Karl Barth said the task of theology was "to apprehend, understand, and speak of God." Isn't that what we all want to do as believers who happen to be involved in the marketplace? We want to hear God, understand God, and speak about God to others both with our voices and our daily activities.

Every time we make a statement about God's involvement in our affairs (something Christians should often do), we are "doing theology." In fact, we *are* theologians!

Once we push the stereotypes aside, we can see theology as more relevant than we thought. Yet too often we associate it with stuffy scholars who do their work in a vacuum. They, meanwhile, may stereotype businessfolk as money-grubbers who go about daily work with nary a thought about the eternal bottom line.

A theologian who doesn't have both feet firmly planted in the realities of everyday life probably isn't worth much in the kingdom of God. But then, neither is the businessperson who never thinks about what faith in God really means to the marketplace we work in.

Like I said, maybe businesspeople and theologians should get together and compare notes.

June

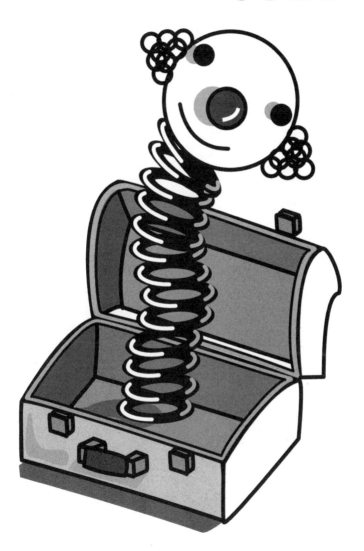

At play in the Word of the Lord

Ever had a prankster in your office? The kind who lets loose every now and then, playing a practical joke? If so, consider yourself lucky.

Sociologists have found that people who have plenty of pride in their work are the most likely to play practical jokes on the job. So the office prankster may in fact be better for the firm than the glowering face that reeks of stolid purpose.

As editor of a magazine dealing with faith in the marketplace, I see a lot of people at work. I've observed that playfulness plays a big role in job satisfaction and effectiveness.

People who see their jobs as a place to exercise the full realm of daily spirituality and discipleship are also the most fun to be around.

Studies show that employees with a sense of humor do a better job. Their productivity is higher, and they spend less time at home sick.

Playful behavior and laughter can trigger beneficial chemical and physiological changes in the body. A good laugh also makes employees more creative.

That's news to those who mistake dourness for diligence, who equate fun with frivolity.

I believe God wants us to have fun, even on the job.

Does the Bible encourage play? It's not a major theme. David didn't compose a psalm to his favorite chariot racer. Paul didn't write a letter to the Troas Red Wings. Still, there's evidence that God is interested in fun.

Psalm 104 suggests that our Maker had a good time creating the world: "He makes the clouds his chariot, and rides on the wings of the wind. . ." (104:3, NIV). God created Leviathan to frolic in the seas (104:26).

The book of Proverbs must come from a playful pen. A sad sack wouldn't write such material: "The lazy person buries a hand in the dish, and is too tired to bring it back to the mouth" (26:15, NRSV).

Even the book of Job, not usually thought of as a fun section of Scripture, gives us a picture of the mountains "where all the wild animals play" (40:20, NRSV).

The perfect society, the city of Jerusalem, is depicted as a place where one can hear the voices of those who make merry (Jer. 30:18-19). Psalm 149:3 speaks of praising the Lord with dancing.

In Ecclesiastes, work and play are affirmed as gifts to be enjoyed.

The Song of Solomon speaks of lovers at play. Something of God is seen in their playful embrace.

Zechariah 8:5 (NRSV) says Jerusalem "shall be full of boys and girls playing in its streets." Some think this is an early reference to street hockey. (I think God prefers baseball. Isn't there something eternal about a game with no clock?)

In the movie *Chariots of Fire*, future missionary Eric Liddell was competing as an Olympic track star. He tells his sister, "I believe that God made me for a purpose—for China. But he also made me fast. And when I run, I feel his pleasure." For Eric Liddell, the sport of running was part of God's acceptable rhythm of life.

The Sabbath rule tells us, *Don't work all the time; take a break!* But the Sabbath is more than just a pause to refresh. Could it also reflect a pattern of God at play?

Nearly all people, given the choice, would rather laugh than cry. That must tell us something about God, in whose image we're made.

When life goes as God intended, there is joy, fun, and laughter.

So why not at work?

Who is my neighbor?

The VW camper had seen better decades. It had a new battery and a terrific sound system, but compression was low in three cylinders. And the body? It was a rust bucket.

I set a price I thought was fair and put a FOR SALE sign in the window.

One serious buyer showed up. As we circled the camper together and poked and revved, I learned that he was a student at a local Bible college and was dating a young woman down the street. I discovered that I also knew his father.

Why did my palms suddenly get sweaty? Was I embarrassed to sell this junker? Maybe deep down I'd hoped some stranger would take it off my hands and never be seen again. This young man, however, was almost a neighbor.

Perhaps he could be talked out of it. I'd wave him good-bye and await more distant prey. I found myself being brutally honest.

"You good at body work? Needs an overhaul, too. Hmmm, is that clutch slipping?"

He was undaunted. It had been love at first sight, blind love.

I was relieved when I encountered the fellow a

year later and learned he was still happy with his purchase. I'd worried that he would hit a pothole and the whole thing would collapse in a heap of rust. If he had been a stranger, I probably wouldn't have cared. Not as much, anyway.

I suppose it's natural though not so noble to care more about a neighbor than a stranger. We've been taught to love our neighbors (Matt. 19:19) and not harm them (Rom. 13:10). Our real motive may be self-preservation; if our product goes sour, we're not anxious to face the victim at the next block barbecue.

Society tells us a "neighbor" is someone nearby, either geographically or socially. Proximity affects how much we care. One of my first lessons in journalism was that people are more concerned about what's close. A single auto fatality in the hometown rates a bigger headline than fifty killed in a bus crash in Peru. A house fire in the suburbs makes the local news but not the network broadcast.

When a lawyer asked Jesus, "Who is my neighbor?" he talked about a good Samaritan (Luke 10:29-37). Most people know the parable; not all grasp its meaning. The real neighbor, we recall, is the one we'd least expect. Not someone who lives next door, not someone of the same social class, not someone who shares a family connection. He is a despised Samaritan, a complete stranger and in some sense even an enemy.

Real neighborliness, the story tells us, means

showing mercy and acting with compassion when there is no conventional social obligation to do so.

Even more important than identifying my neighbor, Jesus says, is the question "To whom am I a neighbor?" His answer widens the definition: "Be a neighbor to anyone who needs your help" (restated).

Only a heel wants to treat a neighbor badly. Friends, family, the folks down the street—we all want to treat them well. But a stranger we'll never see again, or the peasant a world away? That's another story.

Would my dealings be different if every needy person were my neighbor and the whole world my neighborhood?

I'll think about that the next time I sell a car.

Lord of the hoeing

Some of you folks down south are harvesting while here, north of the forty-ninth parallel, we're still busy cultivating.

Nevertheless, the anticipation of harvest, if not its timing, is the same everywhere. Harvest feels good. It has its own energy, smell, and mystique. It marks the end of a process that began long before.

As a boy, I spent many long days, hoe in hand, clawing weeds in the onion fields: Acre after acre of sour-smelling onions. Finish one field, and another is waiting. *Will those onions ever reach maturity? Does the hour hand ever move?*

Yet grow they did. After weeks and weeks of hoeing, coddling, cultivating, spraying, and irrigating, the onions grew bigger than baseballs.

Marvelous things happened at harvesttime. Work became more fun. The onions still reeked, worse than before. Cutting the tops released a flow of juice that infected hands and clothes. Noses burned and eyes dripped. We worked harder and longer than ever. But it didn't matter. It wasn't drudgery because it was *harvesttime*. The fruits of our labors were being plucked from the soil.

The result of our work was there before us, to see,

to weigh, to sell. As the bins filled, our sense of worth and joy welled up within us.

The product even *looked* different during that festive time of year. Behold the onion, no longer a fragile sprout to be sheltered and cajoled, but now a firm and robust bulb, ready to grace hamburger or stew.

The late Stan Mooneyham, longtime crusader for the hungry and dispossessed, once described harvesting as a dramatic and fulfilling part of life's cycle. "You see what you get, and you get what you see," he wrote. "In the earlier stages, there is nothing—or, at least, very little. In fact, when you plant, you cover up even what you started with."

However, those early stages are vital. Without the drudgery of preparing the soil, planting the seed and tending it to maturity, there would be no fulfilling harvest. No stage can be left out.

It is tempting to become preoccupied with harvest. In the church, at least, some are inclined to jump from the sowing to the reaping, to exalt the evangelist who "closes the deal." This can lead to a skewed ranking that overlooks unsung second-string workers and ministries. Without them, no harvest would be possible in the first place.

Hoeing isn't always exciting. Nor is the grueling task of preparing new ground: tearing out stumps, leveling chuckholes, clearing rocks. Bringing in the crop is more fun. Maybe that's why some like to support ministries that can show a full bin *now*, forgetting that somewhere along the way, somebody had to buy the fuel to plant and cultivate.

"I know the Lord told us to pray for workers to be thrust into the harvest," Mooneyham wrote, "but I don't think he'd mind if we broadened it to include some who will cultivate, plant, and hoe. . . . The Lord of the joyful harvest is also Lord of the footslogging and the hoeing."

In business and in the church, we can't all harvest. Somebody has to hoe.

Why Otis stayed unsaved

My landlord, Otis, didn't have much use for the church. He saw it as a waste of time.

Otis thought Christians were phonies. Worst of the lot, in his view, was the local church pastor who also ran a small business on the side. Otis had dealt with him once and felt he'd been cheated.

I knew the pastor. He'd bragged to me about outfoxing clients on business deals. So it wasn't hard to believe Otis's version of the transaction, even without knowing all the details.

"Won't see me in church again," Otis grumbled.

A few years later, Otis passed away. As far as I know, he died an unbeliever.

That was a long time ago. I remembered Otis recently during a discussion of evangelism and ethics. Someone was putting forth the view that evangelism was the primary Christian task, and that other forms of churchly activity were secondary, such as promoting biblical ethics in business.

Of course ethics were important, this person was saying, but the real core of the Christian life was evangelism, telling others about Jesus. You could do all the good you wanted, but it was all for nothing if you weren't explaining the way of salvation.

Otis's case had been precisely the opposite. You could preach to Otis into the wee hours, but it was all for nothing because he already had a real-life image of what Christians were like. His pastor's business ethics had told him all he wanted to know about the Christian faith.

Otis was demonstrating, in reverse, what church-growth research would begin to document years later: The vast majority of new converts are brought to faith not by organized evangelism programs but by friends, family, and positive personal contact with other Christians. Our relationships and behavior in daily life speak louder than any verbal testimony.

What is our purpose on earth? Those who say "to win souls" sometimes tend to make Christian faith into an endless sales pitch, like a pyramid scheme. They give little thought to the "product" being distributed. With a more comprehensive view, we recognize our assigned task to glorify God and bear witness to our new identity as redeemed creatures, in a "new creation" (2 Cor. 5:17, NRSV).

Clearly, there is a vital place for verbal witness. We cannot do without it. Those who bear witness to Christ's redemption in their daily life and work must also be ready "to give the reason for the hope that you have" (1 Pet. 3:15, NIV). But do our verbal witness and our practical witness need to be separated into two camps?

The great commission tells us not only to make

disciples and baptize but also to teach all that Jesus commanded (Matt. 28:19). It calls us to express the totality of his teaching and relationships. This means to love, serve, preach, and heal.

Many of us may not be proficient at verbally explaining the way of salvation. But all of us demonstrate by our relationships and actions whether or not we walk in the light of the resurrection.

Francis of Assisi said it right: "Preach the gospel always. If necessary, use words."

July

A gospel of grit

You've probably never heard a sermon on Proverbs 14:4: "Where no oxen are, the trough is clean; but much increase comes by the strength of an ox" (NKJV).

This doesn't fit our idea of deep theology, but it's quite basic. "Do you want to have a clean manger, a tidy but empty barn? Then don't keep oxen. But if you want a good harvest, you will need those oxen, and your barn will get messy."

This is typical of the book of Proverbs as it comments on the nitty-gritty aspects of life. With unsparing candor, it addresses matters like gossip, sloth, household quarrels, and business. Here are some samples (NRSV):

- How long will you lie there, O lazybones? (6:9)
- Like vinegar to the teeth, and smoke to the eyes, so are the lazy to their employers. (10:26)
- The Lord abhors dishonest scales, but accurate weights are his delight. (11:1)
- "It's no good, it's no good!" says the buyer; then off he goes and boasts about his purchase. (20:14)
- Food gained by fraud tastes sweet to a man, but

he ends up with a mouth full of gravel. (20:17)
• If a man loudly blesses his neighbor early in the morning, it will be taken as a curse. (27:14)

In Proverbs, the sages express earthly and earthy concerns. We see a God with both feet on the ground.

Proverbs is one of a small collection of Old Testament books known as wisdom literature (including Job, Ecclesiastes, and Song of Solomon). Someone has called these writings the "irreligious orphans" of the Old Testament. They seem short on spirituality and long on the grist of daily life. You won't find much there about justification by faith.

However, they deal with other crucial themes. They tell us that human life itself is central to God's interest. They assure us that the routine stuff of our lives is important.

Elsewhere in Scripture, we learn that God has majesty. God is divine. God is righteous. God is the God of our salvation. God is all-powerful.

Books like Proverbs tell us that God is interested in more than doctrine, theology, and religious language.

Wisdom literature grew out of the daily lives, relationships, and struggles of people like you and me. "Anything that occurs in the dwelling place of humans comes under the care, concern, and saving possibilities of its Designer," writes Kathleen O'Connor.

Out of these homespun bits of wisdom comes the serious truth that God is in everything.

God doesn't dip into human life just on Sunday morning and then take off for the rest of the week. God doesn't hibernate for six days and then wander back into our lives on the seventh. God is present in the frantic activity of daily, ordinary existence.

This gospel of grit tells us that the daily grind of the marketplace is more important than we often think.

In short, our work matters to God.

Power in the hands of a few

On a blazing summer afternoon, there's nothing like a wedge of cool, crisp watermelon. And that California day was sauna hot. Around 102 degrees. The watermelons were everywhere, piled up at roadside markets. Sweet, juicy, and thumping-ripe.

However, we couldn't eat them. They weren't for sale.

Some were contaminated. There was no way of telling the bad from the good. So the authorities had banned all watermelons until they could get to the bottom of the problem.

A few growers were to blame. They had used an illegal pesticide, making the melons unsafe to eat. These were a tiny fraction of all growers, but they had spoiled things for the rest. Long after the problem was cleared up, some consumers were still nervous about eating watermelon.

A small minority had managed to tarnish the image of all the growers.

The human memory often remembers the bad and ignores the good. The other week I griped that a certain airline "always lost baggage." Actually, they had lost my baggage twice. On dozens of trips, my suitcase had come through on schedule. But what stuck in my mind was their occasional lapse.

We remember the friend who is misdiagnosed by a physician, but we overlook the many who are healed. We blast the media for yesterday's goof, yet for every error, a thousand facts are reported correctly.

There is much power in the hands of a few.

The reputation of business suffers from the misdeeds of a minority. One national survey showed that only 29 percent of the public felt confident about the business community. My profession, journalism, fared only slightly better in the survey.

These negative images are reinforced on television, where businesspersons are typically seen as shysters, and journalists as ruthless hacks. Christians, if shown at all, come across as self-righteous and phony.

Such images represent the mighty power of a few.

Can that principle work in reverse and be turned to good advantage? What has to happen for fairness, honesty, and compassion to become part of the Christian businessperson's public image?

Robert still remembers the dealer who wouldn't sell him the car he had been eyeing as a teenager. "Can't do it," he said when Robert showed up with cash in hand. "We've just discovered it has a cracked block. You'd have nothing but trouble." That was before the days of consumer protection laws.

Sarah won't forget the months her alcoholic husband spent off the job, their savings squandered. She received a company check every week while he dried out.

Eric still speaks fondly of the savvy executive who intervened with creditors and found a way for him to avoid bankruptcy.

Christians in business have enormous power for good. Their deeds won't always make headlines or alter public opinion polls. But they will surely count in the kingdom scheme of things.

Jesus said a morsel of yeast leavens a whole loaf; a tiny mustard seed grows into a tree so big that birds nest in it.

In other words, there is much power in the hands of a few.

Grocery graces

Grocery shopping, like many of life's unavoidable chores, can be a pain. Or it can be an enlightening religious exercise, producing theological insights.

I don't mean the dazzling array of nature's wonders in the produce section, though cool beds of leeks and Swiss chard can inspire thoughts of Eden on ice. No, I mean the microcosm of human anxiety and vexation you find in the Saturday afternoon convergence of frazzled customers, clumsy pushcarts, long lineups, and exchange of money.

A pushy patron elbows me aside to get the last of the bargain-buster chicken, and I abruptly find myself called to exercise tolerance. I make it to the shelf of 49-cent tuna only to find it bare. *They always run out just when I get here,* I mutter, in no mood for forgiveness.

What about patience? There are lots of chances to put that Christian virtue to work as I navigate a congestion of chrome on aisle 4.

What about kindness? We need gobs of that at any busy supermarket, especially on jostling sale days when you skin your knuckles from a cart collision in front of the macaroni. *When will I learn to keep my hands off the outside rim?*

Wherever crowds of people gather for a mundane but necessary task (especially if it'll cost them money), we have ingredients that can lead to tension, hostility, and anger. We also have golden opportunities to offer a soft answer that turns aside wrath, a "go first" wave that melts a furrowed brow, a smile that creates community.

The line is endless at the checkout stand. *Hmm, those chocolate truffles look good,* strategically located in the path of impulse. Temptations galore. Oh yes, the tantalizing magazines, too, with their screeching headlines of sex and mayhem. *Get thee behind me. . . .*

Over yonder a woman has been pushed out of line by a brazen intruder with a cart heaped to a point of architectural wonder. The gentle victim manages a thin smile and seeks another line. Perhaps she too is practicing her Christian virtues.

I watch the pushy one and decide to time her progress and calculate the net gain of her rudeness. Oh, bitter cup of suffering! The cash register has run out of tape. Worse, it takes forever to locate a new roll and fumblingly thread it through a maze of interlocking rollers. Still it doesn't work! The pushy woman, her cart trembling under its load, fumes as the manager is summoned.

The patient woman, meanwhile, has long since found a new line, paid her bill, and left. There is justice after all. The fruit of rudeness is a providential delay in the checkout line.

My line is a sluggish worm, delayed by a check-cashing foul-up. I am still five carts from my reward. I wonder if I'll make it home before the milk sours. I'm so glad I didn't get ice cream.

A miracle unfolds before my very eyes. From nowhere, surely from on high, a new clerk appears, fresh from her break. She loosens the chain from an idle aisle and sings out in angelic alto, "Help you over here, sir?"

I pull out of my paralyzed line. What relief, what joy! I am being offered the free gift of an open checkout station, totally undeserved.

On this harried Saturday afternoon, I can find no better parable of grace.

Nothing without love

If I speak in the tongues of mortals and of angels, but do not have love, I am a noisy gong or a clanging cymbal. And if I have prophetic powers, and understand all mysteries and all knowledge, and if I have all faith, so as to remove mountains, but do not have love, I am nothing. (1 Cor. 13:1-2, NRSV)

If I am the founder of a wildly successful publicly traded franchising enterprise that employs 8,000 people nationwide and gets mentioned in *Forbes*, but have not love, I am nothing.

If I am known throughout the community as an outstanding leader who can organize and motivate people to achieve the impossible, who can rally people and resources around a common cause, but have not love, I am nothing.

If I am a careful and efficient tiller of the soil who can produce 60-bushel wheat, 150-bushel oats, and 200-bushel corn, but have not love, I am nothing.

If I am the Employee of the Year, rising through the ranks with the greatest of speed and making divisional manager before fall, but have not love, I am nothing.

If I hold memberships on the board of a bank, an airline, an investment firm, a government advisory board, and three church agencies, but have not love, I am nothing.

If I am a writer of critically acclaimed books, many of them bestsellers, and have been nominated for a Pulitzer prize, but have not love, I am nothing.

If I have been named Entrepreneur of the Year by a blue-ribbon panel from the state chamber of commerce, but have not love, I am nothing.

If I am pastor of a vibrant, expanding church with a dynamic community outreach, and I host a weekly television broadcast, hold several conference positions, and chair the local ministerial committee, but have not love, I am nothing.

If I started my own business on a shoestring at the age of 24, and against all odds built it into a $250 million company within five years, but have not love, I am nothing.

If I am a college president who has seen enrollment rise 30 percent and two new buildings built and paid for during my first term, but have not love, I am nothing.

If my company's profit-sharing, ESOP, EAP, and other progressive employment policies have gotten me listed in the Hundred Best Companies to Work for in America, but I have not love, I am nothing.

If I am a tenured professor with a string of research successes, erudite academic publications, and a shot at department chair, but have not love, I am nothing.

If I own a company of a thousand workers, and our ratio of net profits to sales consistently ranks among the top five in the country, but have not love, I am nothing.

If I am known as the most generous person in the community, supporter of myriad church causes and giver of 20 percent of pretax profits to charity, but have not love, I am nothing.

I give you a new commandment, that you love one another. Just as I have loved you, you also should love one another. By this everyone will know that you are my disciples, if you have love for one another. (John 13:34-35, NRSV)

August

Sewage ethics

Like many families in our city, we got hit during the Summer of Floods. We came home one Saturday afternoon to find eighteen inches of sewage in our basement.

That's enough to ruin couches, carpets, and walls, not to mention one's sense of smell. It was a huge mess. Everything had to go.

We were among the fortunate, fully covered, thanks to the vigilance of our friendly insurance agent. He had included sewer backup in our homeowner policy.

Through this experience, we made a lot of new friends. We're now on a first-name basis with insurance adjusters, carpenters, drywallers, carpet installers, and electricians.

We also gained a new slant on ethics.

In our city, seven thousand homes were hit. This area has a lot of finished basements, so the average claim was in the neighborhood of $12,000. For several months, the big topic of conversation was insurance and reconstruction.

Some fly-by-night renovators had a field day. One pair spent an hour disinfecting an elderly couple's woodwork and charged $600. A plumber routinely added $1,400 to the price of each backup valve he installed.

Many of the worst culprits, however, were not tradespeople but individual homeowners who saw their flooded basement as a lucky lottery ticket. A local joke developed:

Question: "What's the hardest part about being flooded?"

Answer: "Getting your old furniture into the basement before the adjuster shows up."

Coffee shops buzzed with stories of those who managed to stick their insurer for an extra grand or two. "My cousin Frank thought he needed a new VCR, so he soaked the old one with a garden hose and added it to his claim." After all, the reasoning went, with nearly $200 million worth of damage in our city alone, what's another few hundred dollars?

Insurance companies had methods of verification. But with so many impatient homeowners to deal with, a lot of hanky-panky slid by.

Disasters have a way of bringing out our best, as we reach out to one another in a spirit of mutual aid. The reverse is also true. Remember the looting after the Los Angeles riots? "We would never do that." Yet . . .

I know from personal experience how easily the tide of greed wells up within. There are only a few short steps from "Whew, thank goodness I'm covered" to "Hmm, how can I squeeze another buck out of . . .?"

Corporations are regularly criticized for ethical lapses, both real and perceived. The smart ones formulate "codes of conduct" so their moral obligations are in view.

Maybe it's time for consumers to do the same thing. A "customer code of ethics" would remind us that morality in business isn't a one-way street.

Someone has said that the soul of a company is the lengthening shadow of an individual conscience. The summer of our flood, we saw a lot of those individual consciences in action. It wasn't a pretty sight.

Me? A bleeding heart?

"How did you turn out to be such a bleeding heart? Didn't you come from a business family?"

The person posing the question to me was saying a "bleeding heart" (someone with a social conscience) has no place in the workaday marketplace. I don't agree. If there's ever a place for a tender conscience, it's in the hurly-burly of daily life.

Now, back to the first question. How *did* I turn out to be a bleeding heart, if in fact I am one?

Just blessed, I guess.

Actually, my parents can share some of the blame. At strategic points in my youth, their actions preached mini-sermons demonstrating that compassion for the poor was fundamental to Christian faith. The sermons were simple and basic. And they stuck.

From Dad: We'd just acquired a dazzling new 1957 Chrysler, blaze yellow with a fierce engine and fins that didn't quit. Such flash was relatively new to us, so this macho hunk of metal was special.

A lot of my adolescent identity was wrapped up in it. To me, our shiny bomb symbolized escape from conservative Mennonite confines and entry into the world of high culture.

Thus I was livid when a grubby-faced kid bashed his bicycle into the side of it, putting a long deep gouge into that gorgeous yellow finish. Anyone who's ever owned a new car knows the pain of first dents.

I drooled with payback anticipation as I fingered the culprit. I expected Dad to be as outraged as I was.

Dad certainly wasn't pleased. But the kid was from the tenements, a few streets over, an island of poverty and broken homes in our sea of upward mobility. They were the kind of people to whom we gave hampers at Christmas.

"No," Dad said, his flush of anger giving way to self-control, "we won't pursue it." The message was clear: we don't squeeze the poor, even when it's our legal "right."

From Mom: About the same time, a single woman in our church had the ill fortune to bear a child out of wedlock. She was excommunicated, in the custom of those days, but she and her new baby kept coming back to services.

That was considered bad form. People in the grip of scandal were expected to disappear, to go else-where. Her continued presence caused no little dis-comfort.

My mother's standards in these matters are as high as anyone's, probably higher. But here was a woman who needed support amid her public shame, and my mother went out of her way to pro-

vide it. In the foyer after church, she'd hover atten-
tively over the child, as only my mother can. Many
others, meanwhile, kept their distance. I got the
message.

Have you noticed how often Scripture talks about
defending the widow, the fatherless, the alien, and
the dispossessed? Today these are single parents,
latchkey kids, refugees, and the unemployed. I
never noticed this in the Bible until I was an adult.
But I didn't have to, because I'd already been
taught that this was part of what it means to be a
Christian.

My parents aren't perfect, but they've preached
some nifty sermons. Some of the best didn't even
have words.

Maybe that's why I'm a bleeding heart.

Our kids should be so blessed.

Shall we whine together?

"Businesspeople are whiners," someone said the other day. "They whine about how the church misunderstands them, doesn't appreciate them, and generally alienates them.

"All that is true," he said, "but they're not the only ones who get treated that way. If they want to complain, they should get in line and wait their turn."

Do people in other fields of work feel misunderstood by the church?

Have you ever heard a bunch of schoolteachers together? They know how to complain. No one understands their need for a summer off to prepare for next year. No one realizes how many evenings they spend marking papers. No one understands why so many of them burn out after twenty years.

Look at professors in Christian colleges and seminaries. When they try to keep abreast of the latest scholarship, they are criticized for importing existentialism, modernism, postmodernism, syncretism, humanism, or some other ism into the classroom.

Let's pity journalists for a moment. They always feel misunderstood. The church doesn't understand why the press can't print more puff pieces to show off the greatness of denominational institutions. It just doesn't grasp why writing with candor is not necessarily "sensationalizing" or "airing dirty laundry."

Artists? They are so misunderstood that they can't even stay in the church. Look how many painters, poets, and musicians end up leaving.

Lawyers? Why, they even have a brand of nasty jokes named after them.

Then there are healthcare workers, civil servants, and others too numerous to mention.

I doubt that you ever heard anyone say, "The church really does a good job of understanding and appreciating my profession."

Maybe we should just complain together: "We are all underappreciated, misunderstood, and alienated."

Here's a thought: Maybe we all should take a few steps in the shoes of another and see if that experience rubs off on the church. (On second thought, aren't *we* the church?)

Imagine an aggressive, can-do capitalist making an earnest effort to understand what makes a reflective intellectual tick.

Imagine a government workplace inspector trying—really trying—to understand why a construction contractor is so frustrated by building codes and safety regulations.

Imagine a union boss grappling with what a new set of contract demands will do to the long-term health of the company.

Imagine a farmer joining an environmental organization to find out why its members are so down on pesticides and fertilizer, or an environmental activist attending meetings of a farmers' organization.

Imagine a CEO thinking long and hard about how it would feel to be downsized onto the unemployment line, with no golden parachute.

Imagine a rich person spending a month living on the equivalent of a welfare check.

Imagine a city manager living as a homeless person for a week.

Imagine spending three days with your pastor and seeing what it's like to plan a service, visit a family in crisis, lead a funeral, attend committee meetings, and prepare a sermon.

Imagine—well, you get the idea. Maybe we need more holy dreamers (Acts 2:17).

Business—a mixed blessing

He was successful and wealthy, owner of a thriving business. When his achievements were praised in public, he blushed and said, "I've been blessed."

It was humble and gracious to chalk it all up to "blessing."

Or was it?

The term has several shades of meaning. One is "to hallow or consecrate," as in "bless this food." Another is "to confer prosperity or happiness," probably what the wealthy executive meant.

It can also suggest "divine approval." If this is what the businessman had in mind, he perhaps was less than modest. Humble people seldom boast that God has bestowed approval on them.

The rich and successful often invoke blessing language to explain or justify good fortune. The poor usually don't. I'm still waiting to hear, "I'm unemployed and broke. God has surely blessed me." It's only natural to link blessing with happy outcomes.

Former U.S. president Jimmy Carter, who since leaving office has become deeply involved with the poor, has made this comment about blessing: "There is a human tendency, of which I am also guilty, to think that because I am rich and secure and influential, I must be especially worthy. God has blessed me because I'm better. It is not easy for people to break out of this shell of self-satisfaction."

If we are going to use blessing language in business, we may want to explore deeper layers of meaning. One of my former seminary professors says that in Scripture "to bless" is to fortify, to enable, to empower.

"Blessing is not some verbal sweetness wafted over the congregation to end the service; blessing is the bestowal of generative powers. When God blesses, God makes productive. To bless is to affirm, but it is more, for to bless is to authorize and simultaneously to enable through empowerment."

Can a business then be blessed? Yes, when its activities are in tune with God's kingdom, when the business strengthens, empowers, and enables people and communities to shape the kind of world God intended. Such businesses will prosper in God's economy and will warrant divine approval.

Dennis Bakke, president of AES Corporation, was asked by a reporter if he saw his company's success as a sign of God's blessing. "We have to be careful when using the term *blessing* to describe financial success and material prosperity," he said.

"The blessing is not so much the abundance brought about by the growth of the company but the extra responsibility in terms of the stewardship of increased resources. In a sense, blessing and burden are mixed in that 'to whom much has been given, much is expected.' The key is greater responsibility rather than greater prosperity for its own sake."

Blessings on you!

How green is my job?

It was a great summer at the cottage. There was plenty of sun. With our long winters, we appreciate all the heat we can get.

Since the lake was lower than usual, we had a huge beach. Too bad it was caused by a drought.

Our cloudless days and sprawling sand came at the expense of farmers. Crops were way down this year. The drop in world grain stocks was the steepest ever, meaning lost momentum in the growth of world food output.

That wasn't all. The dry soil blew away like chaff in the summer wind. Reduced river flows caused hydroelectric power to plummet. Commercial fishing was down. Waterfowl suffered as their nesting areas dried up. Our city's drinking water tasted odd because low water stocks produced more algae and forced heavy chlorination.

We were abruptly reminded of how quickly the capital we take for granted—in this case, water—can dry up, and how close we live to the edge of crisis.

Weather experts didn't agree on whether the drought was the result of the greenhouse effect or merely an unpleasant dip in the natural rhythm of things. We have had droughts before. Yet one indicator was startling: the four driest years of the past century had all occurred during the previous decade. Something strange was happening here on the northern prairies.

Climate is a much bigger deal than pleasant summers and mild winters. Some say the economic and political consequences of climatic change pose a threat second only to that of nuclear war.

We live in a fragile, interconnected system. When crisis hits one sector, others hurt. The environment is groaning from acid rain, nuclear waste, defoliation, seaborne garbage.

Who is to blame for this environmental mess? Just about everyone. Business and industry are obviously major culprits, not only as first-strike polluters but also as architects of a consumer mentality that cries "more, more." Business helped householders crave the convenience of aerosol, plastic foam, and the five-gallon flush.

We've had scares before. There was the fuel shortage of the early 1970s. Then that went away, and we've been driving faster again. Various parts of the country have experienced droughts. How many more warnings will we get? Remember the folksong of the 1960s: "Where have all the flowers gone?" It asked the plaintive question, "When will we ever learn?"

Humanity has made a mockery of the vision presented in Scripture: "The desert and the parched land will be glad; the wilderness will rejoice and blossom. Like the crocus, it will burst into bloom; it will rejoice greatly and shout for joy" (Isa. 35:1-2, NIV). Instead, we see the bloom fading, the land more parched than ever. The shouts we hear are more likely to be moans.

I don't know about you, but I'm going to recommit myself to the greening of my job. Many of us make a stab at being environmentalists at home but forget about the forty hours a week we spend at work. I want to consume less, waste less, spoil less. I want to guard against my workplace using poisonous inks and pouring toxins down the toilet.

The first chapter of the Bible tells us that "God saw all that he had made, and it was very good" (Gen. 1:31, NIV).

I'd like to help keep it that way.

September

We care about the work you do

Labor Day weekend is a great time for churches to think about the jobs of its members. Many churches affirm members for assignments in the congregation, such as Sunday school teachers and deacons. Why not do the same for those who minister beyond the congregation in daily work?

Here are some ways to help your church empower members by saying, "We care about the work you do."

• *Dress up for church.* One church encouraged members to wear their work clothes or uniforms to church on the Sunday before Labor Day. Others brought symbols of their daily work for a special display (tools, computers, date books, mops, bedpans). It was a way to visually offer their daily work to the Lord.

• *Update the church directory.* Suggest that your church list members' occupations alongside the usual information. Such a directory makes it easy to call together members around certain issues, like the church that wanted to gain clarity on issues in public education. It gathered all the church members connected with the education system—teachers, administrators, secretaries, school bus drivers, cafeteria workers, school board members, and PTA leaders.

• *Keep the bulletin board busy.* One church secretary scans community periodicals, clips out mentions of anyone from her church, and posts them on a bulletin board in the foyer. These include job promotions and achievements, anything that shows what people from the church family are doing in their community.

• *Put up photos.* A good assignment for a youth group is to dispatch several amateur shutterbugs to photograph members in their primary places of activity, whether it be a job, a volunteer position, retirement, or homemaking. These can then be mounted on a display or published in the church newsletter, to inform one another and affirm people's daily ministries.

• *Make a worship connection.* Encourage your congregation's worship leaders to include workplace connections when they can. Better yet, locate actual resources yourself. Overworked worship leaders will appreciate the help. Develop your own liturgies and songs if you have skill in those areas.

• *How about a workplace topspin?* Most churches have special missions emphases during the church year. Why not include a workplace topspin? Many missions organizations have an occupational dimension. For example, construction trades have a natural link with Habitat for Humanity. Many other mission thrusts have special needs for healthcare workers, educators, tentmakers, farmers, and print-ers. All of these occupational components can be celebrated in the context of mission.

• *Plan a retreat.* A good way to empower people in a ministry of daily life is through lay retreats that discern individual gifts and callings. For best results, these should be small (no more than 25 to 35 people). The emphasis can be on sharing job-related pressures and understanding how one's life in the workplace can be brought under the lordship of Christ.

Some of the participants will later look back on such a retreat as a turning point in life. Retreats can also lead to forming longer-term fellowship groups around the theme of workplace ministry. These can become entry points for nonbelievers.

Remember, the church's greatest link with the secular world is through the jobs of its members.

Soiling the brain

We all know people in business, at the office, or in church whose minds are unusually fertile. They may not be brilliant or mathematically precise, nor able to memorize with ease. But their minds are lively and inventive. Ideas sprout like new shoots after a spring rain.

Those with fertile minds are like prudent farmers who nurture soil, the seedbed of life.

When we say something is "soiled," we usually mean dirty. That's a bum rap. The thin layer of soil covering much of the earth's land surface is good. Without it, we would find little to eat or to nourish life.

My father and I were passing a field of smoldering grain stubble. The fire had been set to burn off the debris of the previous crop. Then the plow could more easily unzip the soil for next year, saving time and fuel. "A pity," said my father, who had spent a lifetime in farming and agribusiness. "Many farmers do that every year after harvest. But over the long run, it destroys the soil."

"How so?"

"Soil is more than just ground-up rock and mineral matter," he said. "It's a living thing, an intricate organism. It needs fiber, roughage, just like we do. The stubble and crop residue should be worked back into the ground, to give body to the soil and help it retain moisture.

"Soil has to be allowed to rejuvenate," he went on. "If it is overworked, leached, or always sown with the same crop, it loses vitality. Soil needs the humus of decayed organic matter. It needs to be cross-planted with different crops, so that nutrients can be replenished. A farmer may find it easier to sow the same grain year after year and then burn off the stubble. But the soil will eventually lose its character, its ability to produce."

Our minds, likewise, can become tired and dull. Those who never till the mind or turn over its soil will not provide the best seedbed for growth. Our minds grow mushy from hosting identical crops year after year, from indulging in an endless diet of shopworn opinions.

If we never open ourselves up to a fresh approach or new possibility, we develop ruts from following the same arid furrow. Soon the arteries of the mind harden; when moisture does come, it runs off swiftly. Little is retained, for the ruts are hard and crusty.

The mind can also grow listless and sandy. Sandy soil does not hold moisture well. It blows away with the first gust of wind. Turgid gumbo, meanwhile, can be packed too tight so that air cannot circulate. Hardpan minds don't produce lush crops.

Cultivating the mind isn't always easy. It takes effort to seek out a new book or develop a new skill. It takes discipline to turn off the same old talk-show host and try to see another side.

Whether in business or the church, Christ is better served by minds that are carefully groomed and tended, rather than burnt and stale. Paul urged us to "be transformed by the renewing of your minds" (Rom. 12:2, NRSV). Peter said our minds should be prepared for action (1 Pet. 1:13). Thoughtful cultivation, mulching, rotation, and infusion of new ideas—these are the things that make our minds fertile and our work a delight.

Potato pride

I was reared in a family that grew potatoes. I wasn't always proud of that. Today I am.

People sometimes laugh about potatoes. They talk disparagingly about "couch potatoes." Computer nuts are called "mouse potatoes." Little do they know of the potato's honorable history.

I have come to think of potato production as a holy calling. I think God created potatoes for a special purpose.

When I hold a potato in my hand and feel its russet skin, I hear the echo of Scripture speaking across the ages with earthy metaphors of sowers and seeds, of rocky ground, of fields ready for harvest.

We don't know if Moses ever ate a potato. But horticultural historians say that long before he crossed the Red Sea, potatoes were being grown in the Andes of South America. By the time of the Spanish conquest, farmers were producing 3,000 varieties. The potato became the basis for several great Andean empires, mainly because of its nutrition and its high commercial value.

In about 1500, the potato was shipped to Europe; 200 years later it found its way to North America. It has become a major food source around the globe. In developing countries, it ranks only after rice, wheat, and maize.

Potatoes are always affordable, even when prices are relatively high. You never hear anyone say, "Ouch, look at those prices. Guess we'll have to cut down on potatoes."

A field of potatoes produces more food and more nutrition more reliably than the same field planted in grain. The nickname SPUD was originally an acronym in famine-ravaged Ireland for the Society for the Prevention of Unwholesome Diets.

Potatoes also consume less energy than does the production of wheat. They do not produce tooth cavities as readily as grains do.

Scientists say that potatoes contain an enzyme that serves as a natural antidepressant. People who eat more potatoes enjoy greater mental health.

Right now, in September, our harvest crews are running from dawn to midnight, bringing in this year's crop of Pontiacs, Norkotahs, Carltons, Russets, and Yukon Gold. By the time they're done, we'll have several storage buildings filled to bursting. If we're careful with temperature, humidity, and ventilation, we'll have a steady supply to meet local food needs until next summer's crop is ready.

We see this all as a noble and godly enterprise. We like to think that by growing potatoes, we're helping to sustain God's Creation, and thereby doing the work of God. Jesus said, "My Father is still working, and I also am working" (John 5:17, NRSV). By growing potatoes, our family has been a co-creator with God, for God so ordered life on earth as to depend on people in our line of work.

Potatoes help me make a "God connection" with work. I can imagine the biblical writer saying, "God looked upon the field of potatoes and saw that it was good."

Whenever we are tempted to regard our faith as something purely "spiritual," something way up there and out of reach, we can think about the potato. It will remind us that God cares about potatoes, as well as sparrows.

What might it take for you to find a "God connection" in your job? Why not look for the places where God is present in your job or industry? Look for the potatoes in your work life. Find ways in which your work is God's work.

An executive worth his salt

How can you be "salt and light" in your workplace?

Some Christians think the only way to be an authentic witness on the job is to try to convert fellow workers to Christianity. Jesus showed that there is more to faith than the act of persuasion. Jesus spent a lot of time teaching and healing. He ministered to the sick. He brought comfort to the oppressed. His actions pointed to a new way of living.

Christians surely need to be ready to tell others about their life-giving relationship with Jesus Christ. There's an old saying, "When the heart is on fire, sparks will fly out of the mouth."

Nevertheless, many daily actions speak louder than words.

Garry Loewen spent fifteen years as an executive with Air Canada before he went into pastoral ministry. Today he works in employment development with Mennonite Central Committee Canada. While working with Canada's major airline, he found ways to be "salt and light" while achieving the business goals of his job.

He recalls the satisfaction derived from helping to build a significant business. In one case, he signed a

$10 million deal to provide ground-handling services to another airline that earlier had vowed never to do business with Garry's firm. He received satisfaction from seeing productivity and on-time departure performance improve every year for four straight years.

Some highlights were not strictly business. One of them was called Robert.

"He was a first-line supervisor, probably in his mid-fifties," Garry recalls. "Air Canada was in a financial crunch and had developed an early-retirement incentive program for its management staff. My corporate obligation in that situation was to try to convince as many of my long-service management employees as possible to seriously consider retirement under this incentive program.

"One day Robert's immediate boss came to me to report that Robert would probably be accepting the package. I knew that the only person still at home in Robert's family was his wife, and that she was dying of cancer. She only had a few months left to live.

"So I called Robert into my office and told him that I didn't think he should accept the package. I said, 'You know there is going to be a lot of upheaval in your life in the next few months, and you're going to need some sources of stability. Let this company be one of those sources.'

"After his wife died, Robert and his children were enormously grateful for that advice. And I was full of joy that on at least this occasion, I had had the wisdom to set aside the objectives of the business and do what was right for one human being."

Perhaps without realizing it, Garry was being a pastor, even while working for a "secular" company.

He was also working for social justice. He participated in corporate programs to improve the quality of the employees' work life, to break down some of the hierarchical barriers in the company, and to restore some dignity to workers at the bottom of the hierarchy by letting them take part in decision-making.

"And," says Garry, "I remember the effort we put into trying to make air travel more accessible to the handicapped—not because of the additional revenue this would bring to us (it wouldn't have been worth the effort for the revenue alone), but because we saw it as one way we could contribute to the building of a more just society."

For Garry Loewen, the daily work of being an executive provided plenty of opportunities to be salt and light by showing Christian compassion.

Garry believes that Christians in the workplace are called to the "parts per million" game where minute traces of certain elements exert enormous influence as catalysts for change. "That," he says, "is what we are called to be like—a people who have an impact on this world that is completely disproportionate to our size or numbers, a people who give to creation its taste and flavor."

October

SUN	MON
1	2
8	9

First-aid ethics

This is World Series month, the time of year when I stay close to the television set. I just saw a classic rundown play between first and second. It was exquisite to see the shortstop back up second and the pitcher back up first with fluid precision. They made it look easy.

Yet of course it wasn't. They don't concoct a strategy on the spot. They know just how to move because they have rehearsed this sort of thing over and over again. Months of practice and season play have honed their skills razor sharp. Their reflexes only seem subconscious.

They are like the company that faced an ethical dilemma forced on them by outsiders. The executives did not spend a lot of time wringing their hands in uncertainty. Long ago they had cultivated a Christian understanding of their work and had set it out in a written code of ethics. They were able to act swiftly to redress the problem and minimize the hurt to all concerned. Like the baseball infielders, they were prepared for exactly such a situation.

Not all corporate executives are so well prepared. Many companies, even those owned by Christians, don't bother to clarify their moral foundations. The owners and key employees may be sincere. But will their faith instantly furnish the solution to a difficult situation? Instincts can falter in periods of high stress. Better to take time, in advance, to flex the muscles that undergird our conduct in the workplace.

The heat of the moment is not ideal for this. In my era, ethicist Vernard Eller advised young people that the backseat of a car (cars were much bigger then, and backseats had a particular reputation) was no place to make moral decisions. Those should have been made earlier. In the passion of the moment, ethical judgments are too easily set aside. This is true in business, too.

Business Week magazine once noted that some major companies caught with their hands in the cookie jar had suddenly "found religion." They would call in an organization that helps businesses develop corporate codes of ethics.

The magazine questioned the validity of a code of ethics that is "hastily patched together . . . simply to counteract bad publicity." It urged companies to consider "cultivating a concern for ethics before trouble strikes, one that reaches beyond routinely handing out a booklet of corporate commandments."

When I was a child I first understood Christianity—incorrectly, I later discovered—as a set of rules and restrictions. I did not immediately grasp that the Christian life had more to do with a relationship and a direction.

In the workplace, as in the faith, rules have their place, but they are not enough. Christian principles in business are more than an ethical first-aid kit that is stored on a company's shelf till crisis strikes. Ethics are not bandages to be slapped onto an injury.

Ethics work best when they are woven into the fabric of workplace life. That should come naturally for the people of God, both in and out of business, who always want to "do what is right and just" (Prov. 21:3, NIV).

The Monday connection

Someone said the other day that the Christian church in North America isn't gaining in size; it's just growing fast enough to keep up with the population.

If true, that isn't encouraging. With all the energy and dollars spent on the "church growth industry" (crusades, broadcasts, books, and seminars), you'd think the church might boost its market share.

National polls, meanwhile, point to a big jump in the number of people experiencing spiritual awakening. In the United States, for example, more people claim commitment to Jesus Christ, but fewer of them are attending church. Not a good sign.

Why has church growth stalled? Former Bethlehem Steel executive William Diehl blames the "Sunday-Monday gap." Too few people connect their faith life with their work life, he says in his book, *The Monday Connection*.

This is not because they are lazy Christians, he says, but because they receive little church help in making the connection. And churches don't give this kind of help because "lay ministry" is misunderstood. Instead of seeing lay ministry as empowering believers to minister in their daily lives (which for working folk usually means the job site), it is seen as getting laypeople more involved in church activities.

For example, courses in "the ministry of the laity" typically deal with how to recruit, train, and support laypersons for volunteer work within the congregation, Diehl says. "Far less frequent are the courses on how to affirm, equip, and support laypersons for ministries in their places of work, their communities, and their families."

Diehl cites a survey that asked evangelicals what they desired most from their churches: 67 percent said they wanted to learn how to apply faith to daily life, and only 17 percent said they wanted more opportunities to be leaders in church. "In short, lay people are hungry for ministry in their daily lives, not in the church."

Yet churches often fail to equip their members for these ministries. For years, Diehl experienced this spiritual schizophrenia. On Sunday his church called him to be a disciple of Christ in the world but gave him no help in how to do it. "My Sunday experience had no connection with my Monday world."

Some churches fear lay ministry will detract from institutional church life. Diehl counters that laypeople who minister in their work actually become better church members. "I have never found a congregation that was sincerely committed to helping equip its people for ministry in daily life that was not a vital, active, purposeful, and growing community of faith. Not a single one. Not in twenty years."

Pushing the Monday connection, then, can benefit the church in two ways. First, it will magnify the ministry of the church. Congregations will minister through their members all week long in exactly that area of life where working adults spend the bulk of their time.

Second, it will help the church grow by giving it the relevance it deserves. Pollster George Gallup has found that people are hungering for the means to relate the experiences of life to their faith. If churches can meet this need, he predicts, there can be real church growth in the next century.

A hiding place of gray

Anyone familiar with the photography of Ansel Adams knows the brilliance of black and white. Even in an age of full-process color, when computers and photocopiers produce the entire spectrum, an Adams creation shows the power of black and white to express mood, drama, and depth.

Editors of publications that still function in black and white know what black ink can do on white paper. When we choose photos for publication, we're looking for a blend of snappy whites, crisp blacks, and muted shades of gray. A picture in pure black and white does not reflect reality. Grays are needed for tonal accuracy.

However, there is such a thing as too much gray. I remember an editor who could demolish a photographer's offerings with a snarly one-liner: No depth of field; poor composition. Or, too gray.

Gray is an important color of the palette. But it must be used sparingly, appropriately, without being overdone. A photograph that is too gray is wimpy, ho-hum. It lacks life, movement.

Now jump with me from the world of photography to that of ethics, especially business ethics. How many times do we hear, "That's not a black-

and-white issue. It's gray."

Often it is. But do we too often hide behind the wall of gray? It can be a defense mechanism to avoid the effort of clarifying what is really right or what is wrong. Whenever an ethical decision is difficult, we can spare ourselves the hard work of determining the right by saying, "It's a gray area."

What do we mean by gray, anyway? My dictionary defines gray as "dull in color," "dismal, gloomy," and "neutral." What do we mean, then, when we speak of a "gray area" in ethics? Probably not dull or dismal. More likely we mean "neither black nor white." In other words, a gray area is one in which there is no right or wrong. It is a neutral area, an ethical free zone.

Ethical issues are often elusive, thorny, and difficult. The right thing to do is not always immediately clear nor readily within grasp. But that does not make the issue neutral, or gray. It simply makes it elusive, thorny, and difficult. It does not unhook us from the responsibility of persistently seeking the truth of a situation and then responding appropriately.

A resolve: Next time I am tempted to call something an "ethical gray area," I will stop first and take stock. Is it really gray, or is that a cop-out because I am unwilling to go to the effort of discerning the actual blackness or whiteness? Have I thoroughly examined the issue in the light of Scripture and the corporate wisdom of the church? Have I exhausted all possible means of analysis? If I call it gray, do I mean unclear, or do I mean it is a neutral issue? Do I have any nagging guilt over this issue? If so, why?

I have before me an Ansel Adams print. With few shades to work with, he manages to produce an image of majesty, movement, conviction. Sure, there are tones and subtle shadings that are not 100 percent black. But the gray is bold, purposeful, deliberate.

Not wimpy.

The CEO as pastor

Did you ever notice how often the term *CEO* comes up in describing pastoral styles? The other day it surfaced in a book on church leadership. There was a section devoted to "the pastor as CEO." It wasn't flattering.

Do some pastors behave like chief executive officers? Should they? A pastor who is a dynamic, energetic leader and strives for measurable goals would be described by some in CEO terms. On a more critical note, the label might also be applied to an autocratic pastor who is obsessed with being in control.

A church periodical recently complained about churches that "follow business models." In many cases, it said, an "employer-employee" attitude has crept in. Pastors talk more openly than they used to about salary and benefits. They'll stop short, though, of calling themselves "hired," still preferring to be "called." But when their services are abruptly terminated, they feel "fired" like anyone else.

There are times when pastors would like to be treated like CEOs, such as when a church decides to "un-call" them. They would like to have the golden handshake that many departing executives manage to arrange no matter how meagerly the company fared on their watch.

Do CEOs get a bum rap in these comparisons? They seem to be stereotyped as dictators who have nothing better to do than bark orders. Is that a fair description of a CEO's work? Maybe it's time to turn the tables and discover how CEOs sometimes behave like pastors, rather than the other way around. Don't they have much in common?

• Like a pastor, a CEO is usually held accountable for the performance of the organization, regardless of where any fault may lie. A CEO will be blamed by the stockholders if the desired rewards aren't forthcoming. "Where's our dividend?" isn't far from "We aren't being fed."

• The best CEOs, like the best pastors, are servant leaders. They get things done by serving others and empowering them. They don't need to use force to bring out the best in people.

• The CEO sets the moral tone for the corporation. No matter how many mission statements or codes of conduct a company may have, it is top leadership that sets the example. No one believes a code of ethics if the people at the top don't model it first.

• CEOs have to do a lot of hand-holding. They may not be trained counselors, but they get to hear a lot of woes, not to mention bickering. Through it all, like a good pastor, they have to remain evenhanded and maintain confidentiality.

• They share leadership with others. If they have any sense, good CEOs will delegate and share responsibility rather than do it all themselves. They know that a big ego will burn out quickly. They are like a good pastor who grasps that the real work of the church is done by the members in cooperation and teamwork.

Having said this, there's still one more way in which CEOs could be like pastors: they, too, should see their work as an assignment from God. Wouldn't it be great if CEOs could say without blushing that they were "called" to their work?

Going a step further, imagine that churches commissioned CEOs and other businessfolk for workplace service. Imagine that churches commissioned all their members for service in daily life. Those churches would probably soon be bursting at the seams. Then they'd have to expand. Before you know it, they'd be building new premises or planning a branch operation.

Just like a CEO.

November

A hand of welcome

I like friendly people. I like friendly clerks. I'll go out of my way for a warm reception. Call me insecure, but I'd rather have a friendly clerk than the lowest price in town.

I visited an electronics store recently. I was pretty far out of my element, so the last thing I wanted was a frosty reception. But the proprietor, busy setting up a display, seemed to resent the intrusion. I backed out rather fast. It's hard enough to spend money on a big purchase; sullen service just makes it worse.

The store down the street welcomed me warmly. The shopkeeper kindly fielded my ignorant questions and chatted with me. He made me feel at home.

Do you want to guess which store got my business?

One of the shops has since gone bankrupt. Want to guess which one?

Folks in the retail and sales trade have learned something about being friendly. They know how to make a visitor feel welcome.

This probably applies to businesspeople in general. They're acquainted with marketing, with putting a client at ease. That doesn't mean they're basically friendlier than other people. But they know how to put their best foot—or hand—forward. They know how to schmooze, and schmoozing isn't all bad.

Now let's switch gears for a moment and think about how we receive newcomers on Sunday morning. Is your church known for being friendly and warm, or for being cold and impersonal?

Years ago when our family moved to a new city, we spent some time "church shopping." One congregation seemed to overflow with hospitality. When we analyzed our reception, we realized that only four people had actually gone out of their way to welcome us. But that was enough to leave a flavor of friendliness. It only took a few.

Most churches are friendly, . . . when you get to know them. But they don't always let it show up front. Many visitors won't wait around to find out. Like the ad says, "You don't get a second chance to make a first impression."

Being outgoing doesn't come easy to everyone. My Mennonite background, for instance, has made a virtue of stoic reserve, as if it somehow equals spiritual humility. The "quiet in the land," as we have sometimes been known, don't always like to extend a hand. Yet we manage to do it in business.

Here's a modest proposal. What if everyone reading this book made a point of being an unofficial "greeter" at church? It's not hard; just keep an eye out for newcomers and give them a hearty welcome. It doesn't take long. Then watch for a return on the investment, beyond your own emotional high. For some visitors, it could turn into a life-changing experience.

Remember, it doesn't take many friendly persons. And maybe the habit will rub off on others.

Blueprint from above

This time of year the Manitoba chill starts to bite, and we all get ready to hunker down for winter. Some of us procrastinators are finally getting around to checking our furnaces and sprucing up the weather-stripping around our doors and windows. Winter here is long and harsh.

I ponder my dwelling and its ability to withstand temperatures of minus 30. I'm reminded of Perry Bigelow, a Chicago housebuilder who puts up highly energy-efficient homes so his customers don't have to pay an arm and leg for heating fuel. His company guarantees that heating bills will not exceed $200 a year. That gives me a sense of comfort. I've worked in Chicago and felt its icy blasts.

Bigelow sees his work as a form of Christian mission. He often imagines a construction company managed by Jesus, and then tries to manage his company accordingly.

For one thing, he strives to capitalize his business responsibly so that his employees have steady work. He sees this, too, as following what Jesus would have done. By aiming for careful, sustainable growth, Bigelow's company was able to withstand the last dip in the housing cycle without laying off anyone, a time when other builders were cutting staff by 50 to 70 percent.

I once heard the late Marlin Miller, a seminary president from Indiana, tell a convention of builders that they were in an excellent position to be Christian peacemakers. He said the biblical vision of peace went further than mere avoidance of conflict. The Hebrew word *shalom* also meant justice and righteousness. People in the construction industry, he went on, could work toward peace in the following ways:

• *By seeking harmony with the natural environment.* The King James rendering of "have dominion" has often been misunderstood to mean "license to conquer," Miller said, when in fact it more correctly means to be a steward and caretaker. For builders to be peacemakers means to establish and maintain peace with God's created order. The implications are far-reaching, such as avoiding the temptation to overbuild.

• *By caring about the poor.* Scripture often measures justice by what is happening to the needy. Christian builders can use their power and resources to obtain justice for the poor in the area of housing.

• *By considering the welfare of the wider human community.* This can mean studying the social impact of housing styles. High apartment density, for example, can cause psychic trauma to local dwellers. A builder concerned with biblical justice might refuse a sardine-can project.

• *By seeking peace in their workplace.* They monitor their use of power in employer-employee relationships. They create the kinds of work situations that make peace possible. Bigelow casts this same theme in the Bible's language of "body." In his company, he says, "each person's work is integrated and interrelated with the work of others, and there is a high level of respect for each person's contribution."

Both Bigelow's and Miller's concerns address the same basic issue: How would Jesus function in my business? In my work, I can pose a similar question: What kind of magazine would Jesus edit?

You can ask the same in your field of work.

Explosive profit

The other day someone lobbed a grenade into a discussion about Christian business ethics. The grenade was called "profit." Another person couldn't resist pulling the pin, and in a few seconds the grenade went off with a huge fuss, hurling shrapnel in all directions.

One side equated profit with profiteering. The other countered that if businesses didn't make a profit, they couldn't provide jobs.

I found myself caught in the middle. I don't like it when people are gouged. But neither do I think profit is a dirty word. I have a problem with those who righteously label all profit as evil.

Profit, writes John Rudy, "simply identifies the gain we hope to realize by selling a product or service for more than it costs. Without gain, we can't be in business very long, just like a teacher or nurse can't work for free very long."

Whatever our rhetoric, don't most of us believe in some form of profit? In business or in households, what comes in must exceed what goes out. Otherwise, we have a problem. Not many people are willing to receive less pay than what it costs to live. We all want to make our own form of surplus, or profit.

Few of us have clean hands. Most of us, whether in business or not, want to maximize our own financial position in any transaction. We want to get the best deal. When we shop for a car, we want to haggle the price down low. When we sell a house, we list it as high as possible. We want to take advantage of market increases and sell for as much as we can. That's simply the consumer's version of the free-market maxim "what the market will bear."

As important as profit is, I have a problem with businessfolk who laud it as a corporate deity that justifies greedy behavior. Quite simply, profit is not the goal of a business, any more than the goal of a decent politician is to get elected.

Isn't it better and more Christian to recognize that the aim of a business is to provide goods and services that help humanity? Christians in business use the skills and resources God has given them to help sustain humanity's need for food, shelter, clothing, transportation, entertainment, and so on. That makes them, in a sense, co-creators with God. They become God's "junior partners."

Profit is necessary for a business to carry out its social role of providing jobs and sustaining the fabric of this world. But for a "minister of commerce," profit is not the chief goal.

Max De Pree, former head of Herman Miller, Inc., compares profits to breathing. We need air to breathe, he contends, and we need profits to continue in business. But none of us would say our mission as humans is to breathe. We don't come to the end of the day and say, "Hey, I'm still breathing, so it must have been a great day." We are familiar enough with the world of medicine to know that people can be kept alive on a respirator even though they have no real quality of life.

David Fagiano, former CEO of the American Management Association, has written that "any company in business to make money will soon be out of business. Profit is not the mission of any company that wants to be around for the long haul.

"Companies exist to make something or provide a service. Profit is the byproduct of this activity. When profit is your mission, decisions become increasingly short-term. The organization moves in ever smaller concentric circles, until it eventually collapses on itself and disappears" (*Management Review*, Sept. 1991).

That was no left-wing radical speaking; that was an avid free enterpriser.

Business guru Kenneth Blanchard has written that managing only for profit is like playing tennis with your eye constantly on the scoreboard. Not only won't the game be fun, but you won't play as well, either.

What if . . . ?

Every now and then, we hear of companies getting into trouble for stretching the truth in advertising. The ad watchdogs work hard to ensure that we aren't sold a false bill of goods. Producers of mouth-wash can't say their product "kills cold germs" if they can't prove it. Ice-cream look-alikes without any real ice cream have to be called "dairy-flavored treats." And reconstituted orange juice can't be called "freshly squeezed."

What if "truth in advertising" were spread a bit further into the world of business? What if, of all things, it extended to doublespeak?

You know about doublespeak. It used to be the private preserve (native tongue?) of bureaucrats. They're the folks who gave us "revenue enhance-ment" instead of "taxes," and replaced "killing" with "unlawful deprivation of life." A new art form was reached when the Pentagon spent $2,000 for a "hexaform rotatable surface compression unit." It turned out to be a 16-cent nut, to fit on a bolt.

When someone is described as "motivationally de-ficient," that means lazy. And if our company goes through "a permanent negative adjustment" or a "fourth-quarter equity retreat," you can bet it's time to update that résumé because a "work-force imbalance correction" or "release of resources" may be looming, and we could be "vocationally relocated."

Doublespeak is corrupting and manipulative, says Rutgers professor William Lutz, author of a book on the topic. At its worst, it is language designed to limit or even eliminate thought. At its least offensive, it is language that distorts by inflating the importance of the insignificant or by minimizing the importance of the significant.

What if businesses weren't allowed to use doublespeak? What if they were legally forbidden from using sanitized labels like "downsizing" and "rightsizing" and had to say instead, "We're dumping employees"?

What if the burger chain were forbidden to say (as one did) that it was finally going to reveal the ingredients of its fast-food because of "increasing consumer interest"? What if it had to admit plainly, "We are being pressured by the attorneys general of three different states. . . ."

Imagine the church being included in the new truth-telling blitz. Instead of reporting, "We are more concerned with quality than quantity," the church might say at its annual business meeting, "We had another membership loss last year."

The upwardly mobile pastoral candidate could no longer say, "I feel led to accept your invitation to a wider and more fruitful ministry," but would have to acknowledge, "I'd love the chance to lead your large and wealthy church."

Such a regulation would put a crimp into some door-to-door visitation programs. Instead of claiming to be conducting a "religious survey," a "truth in religion" doctrine would require door-knockers to say, "I'd like to get my foot in the door long enough to plug our church."

Editors' rejection slips would have to be rewritten. Instead of telling the writer (as I have been told), "We are temporarily overstocked with this type of material," the rejection slip might have to say, "These kinds of articles are a dime a dozen." Instead of saying, "We feel your article does not meet the current needs of our readers," it might have to read, "Sorry! We think your article just isn't very good."

What if a Christian commitment to honesty and "speaking the truth in love" governed all public communications of both business and the church?

What if . . . ?

December

What's the real cost?

Call me slow, but I had never heard the term "full-cost accounting" until a few years ago. It is a mystery how I survived so long without it.

The other day I had a chance to use it. In a discussion of a business proposition that had some risks involved, I heard myself saying, "Let's look at the full costs of this."

Actually, I've known the theory, if not the terminology, since youth. When I bought my first new car, my father patiently explained that there would be other costs besides gas and oil. There would be insurance, registration, upkeep, and—the big one—depreciation. So a weekend trip became more than just a few tanks of gas. Full-cost accounting produced the hidden horror of several extra cents per mile.

Many of us who are associated with business know about full-cost accounting. We know what goes into the price of a product, at least the tangible costs of design, materials, labor, storage, marketing, transportation, and so on.

Not all of us practice real true-cost accounting, however. We may calculate our own direct expenses without figuring the social cost to other stakeholders who may also pay a price. Employees pay a price for unfair, unhealthy, and hostile work environments, such as when supervisors yell at them or harass them. The family of an employee pays a price if workplace stresses and irritations are brought home. Other taxpayers pay a price if the business receives subsidized support services. The community and future generations pay a price if effluents are not disposed of properly.

In his book *Small Decencies*, John Cowan tells of a corporate officer who casually said he'd have to dump a few divisions to get his company back on course. Whoa! Dump a few divisions? But what about the hordes of employees who would be thrown out of work? Cowan writes,

> How many pregnant women would hear that their husbands no longer had health insurance? How many young men and women would have to change their choice of colleges? How many bicycles would not be bought for Christmas? How many families would have to try to live on a welfare check? How many men would struggle not to think of themselves as useless? How could a perfectly nice man, a well-mannered gentleman, fail to factor these elements into his assessment of the situation?

Like many of us, this corporate officer didn't bother to consider the effects on others who found themselves caught in the lengthening shadow of his actions.

An outplacement executive recently complained that some firms are now paying the price for their layoff binge of a few years ago. He said the passion to be lean produced "corporate anorexics" whose creative juices have dried up. Somewhere, full-cost accounting was neglected.

A long time ago, Jesus talked about "counting the cost." Interestingly, he used a business illustration. "Suppose one of you wants to build a tower. Will he not first sit down and estimate the cost to see if he has enough money to complete it?" (Luke 14:28, NIV). The message to his disciples was that the cost of following him might be higher than they thought.

Of course, Jesus didn't really mean business.
Did he?

Oom-pah-pah

The front of the Christmas card showed an awkward beast blowing into a huge, unwieldy brass instrument. Above the shiny bell hung three mundane quarter notes separated by a number of two-beat rests, as in "oom-pah-pah." As a former dabbler in music I could see this wasn't much of a melody.

Inside, the message continued: "This has been the tuba line of the full-orchestra version of 'Joy, joy, joy.' "

In its own breathy and monotonous way, even the lowly tuba was expressing what it could of the season's excitement.

We used to laugh at the tuba, that big brass toilet bowl that seemed most at home in the marching band or polka crowd. Other instruments had more class, we thought. The really clever musicians played the strings. It took more talent and hard work, but at least string players got to perform all the time. Then there was the flute, or oboe or bassoon. Those were tough instruments, the "musical ones."

Even my own choice, the trumpet, was a notch above the tuba. After all, we trumpeters played the arresting fanfares and other stuff you could at least recognize. And though fellows like Mozart didn't write much for us, at least we had our day during Handel's *Water Music,* or, if we were really good, "The Trumpet Shall Sound" in *Messiah.*

But the tuba? Who cared about the tuba?

Then I played in an orchestra with an outstanding tuba player. I could never figure out why Brent had picked such an instrument. Nothing classy was ever written for it. Who'd ever heard of a tuba concerto?

Brent didn't seem to mind. He would warm up with lightning runs, trills, and arpeggios, and finish off with a tuba solo that would make our spines tingle. Then, during rehearsal and performance, he would settle back and contentedly puff away on his bass notes, providing harmonic support for the rest of us.

When we played in concert, the audience never got the full benefit of Brent's virtuosity. They saw him, to be sure. How could you miss that imposing mass of burnished metal. But all they heard were his undergirding tones. Later, over tea, they wouldn't praise his great tuba work. They'd talk about the flawless woodwind passage, or the great cello obbligato, but the tuba? Nary a mention.

Brent knew he'd rarely, if ever, get the accolades that came to the strings, the French horns, and even the timpani. But he persisted, blissfully unconcerned with personal glory. He was content to be part of the whole, the total sound. He was a team player.

So Brent kept playing his notes with dedication and without much evident fanfare. Most of the listeners didn't realize how much he was contributing. They didn't know how much they'd miss with him not there. They weren't aware of how badly they needed his rhythmic beat, his understated runs.

However, Brent knew. And so did the conductor, the man who had in front of him the master score, the complete story with all its related components.

How nice, I think now, that we have tuba players in the family of God. People who do their work day in and day out, contributing where they can with ability and strength. Teachers, plumbers, businessfolk, cooks, flight attendants, nurses, letter carriers, clerks, and bus drivers. People who help us maintain the framework of our song, even though they seldom get to solo.

Do you hear
what I hear?

Christmas is sometimes called the season of good news. But is it good news for everyone?

What exactly was the news at the first Christmas? We get an inkling of it in Mary's song (Luke 1:46-55, NRSV). Mary has been pondering her strange pregnancy. Here she is, a woman of "low estate," a nobody, and God has exalted her for this important role. Mary, in deep contemplation, composes this song:

> My soul magnifies the Lord. . . .
> He has looked with favor on the lowliness
>   of his servant. . . .
> He has scattered the proud. . . .
> He has brought down the powerful from their
>   thrones, and lifted up the lowly.
> He has filled the hungry with good things,
>   and sent the rich away empty.

Here, within the womb of this woman of low estate, is the concrete realization of God's purpose.

God is going to overthrow the proud, the mighty, and the powerful. He's going to send the rich away empty-handed. The rules of the world are being thrown out. What's happening here is not just the birth of a baby, but a complete reversal of human values.

And this is supposed to be good news?

Like most news, it all depends on your perspective. For the rich and powerful, Mary's song presents a worrisome prospect. For the poor and oppressed, it's terrific news.

Some people would like to spiritualize Mary's words because they seem so incredible. And yet, maybe they mean exactly what they say.

Imagine being poor in Palestine and hearing Mary's song. This is what you might hear:

> The kingdom of God is the kind of place where those who are rich will share. The kingdom of God is the kind of place where those who have power will step off their thrones and no longer oppress. The kingdom of God is the kind of place where people who have influence will take the risk of intervening on your behalf.

In other words, the kingdom of God is an upside-down kingdom.

If you are one of the oppressors, this is not good news. For those whose self-esteem is found in thrones, Christmas is not really a time to sing "Joy to the World." For those whose joy is found in wealth, the incarnation is not an event to gladden the heart. The temptation of our world is to be sucked into empty power and empty thrones, to want to become precisely the kind of people Mary says will be brought down.

How would things look in our workplaces if we modeled the upside-down kingdom? Have you ever wondered what it would be like to have a manager's performance evaluated by those lower on the ladder rather than by those above? What if we gave equal respect to a competent janitor as to a vice-president? What if there were no feelings of discrimination based on gender, age, or race? What if the gap between the lower-paid workers and the CEO began to narrow rather than continually widen?

Now that would be an upside-down workplace.

Christmas brings good news for some, and bad news for others.

It's our choice as to which it will be for us.

A parable of rude awakening

I knew it was going to be a long day when I took my number from the dispenser. The immigration office was jammed with people holding little numbered slips, the kind you get at some meat markets. I remembered all the stories about being treated like a number. Mine was 52. They were serving number 24.

There was no place to sit because there were too many other people who had business to do. Mexicans, Hmongs, Laotians, East Indians, Egyptians, Lebanese, and a few Americans.

Mothers and fathers and uncles and grandmothers waited, clutching little numbers in one hand, and a swatch of documents in the other. Toddlers crawled on the gritty floor. Infants whimpered, old men coughed, noses dripped. Pores oozed sweat as the day wore on. We were here to do business in this place of power. This place of red tape, runarounds and, as it turned out, rudeness.

An Indian couple's number was called. The clerk greeted them with curled lip. Apparently their rope of red tape was not quite long enough; they needed yet another document.

"But this is all you gave us yesterday," they tried

to plead in mangled English. It didn't matter; the machine would have to expectorate more tape. The clerk's abusive words stabbed like icicles. She seemed to enjoy her power. These weren't people to her. They were, truly, just numbers. Their personal plights meant nothing to this soured worker, who had forgotten how to serve.

The couple struggled to contain their rage, as did the rest of us who still had numbers in our fists, who still had to face the dragon lady. The couple left, humiliated and powerless against this hostile, immovable machine. Tomorrow, for the nth day in a row, they would traipse back, their gait a little slower, their heads and shoulders drooping a little lower. They would take another number, and then they would wait.

Outside, jolly carols filled the streets. What a contrast! Or was it? Would Jesus have come to this hostile place? He had, in a manner of speaking, been here before. He came, after all, during a census. A bureaucracy had flexed its muscle and thrown all the world into turmoil.

Joseph and Mary could tell us a few things about runarounds, about painful treks from inn to inn with birth pangs coming on. They may have resembled the Indian couple, their hopes shucked into disarray.

They knew frustration, helplessness, alienation. They knew the slam of the door. "Not tonight. Come tomorrow, and bring more tape." They would have recognized the dragon lady's timeless snarl.

Such was the world that greeted Jesus, no less grimy and angry than the office where people take numbers and await abuse. He had come to this unfriendly place to rescue all these people—the stooped Mexican patriarch, the student from Iran, the bewildered Hmong couple, the Lebanese executive, the furtive refugee from Central America—all victims of spiritual as well as political indifference. These were the people with whom Jesus identified when he came among us to bring deliverance from the grip of bondage and oppression. He brought that to them. And he is bringing that to all of us.

Even, I grudgingly conceded, to the dragon lady behind the counter.

I fondled my little number 52. They were now up to 25.

Christmas was coming to this dingy office.

Shaping up

My friend Al is a potter and makes miracles with his hands. Give him a wad of clay, and he'll pat and squeeze it into a lovely bowl.

His craft brings up a vivid spiritual image, one you've seen on Christian posters and book jackets. We too, the image goes, are shapeless blobs that can be molded into something beautiful. In God's hands, we are raw lumps, ready to be pressed, kneaded, and fired into well-contoured vessels.

Part of the sequence is sometimes missed. We don't always see the wayward lump that sprouts a defect and has to be pounded back down to start afresh.

Remember the prophet Jeremiah? The people of Israel had sinned, and God had a message for them. He sent Jeremiah to the local pottery shop. There he

found the potter working at his wheel. But the jar that he was forming didn't turn out as he wished, *so he kneaded it into a lump and started again.* Then the Lord said: O Israel, can't I do to you as this potter has done to his clay? As the clay is in the potter's hand, so are you in my hand. (Jer. 18:2-6, LB, italics added)

Ah, persistence! When the potter sees a problem on the wheel, the vessel can be squeezed back and begun anew. When we don't shape up, God can stop the wheel and pummel us back down. As long as the clay remains supple and willing, it can be coddled and cajoled into the desired shape. God doesn't throw us out.

Think on this during these last days of December as we segue out of the season that says, "God with us."

The year is almost over; for some, not a minute too soon. We didn't all have a great year.

Some of us lost jobs, experienced financial distress, or watched a company go down the tubes.

Maybe we suffered moral lapses, sickness, doubts, or emotional defeats.

Many of us in some way betrayed ourselves, our families, our companies, our churches, our Lord.

We lied, cheated, gossiped, hated, or behaved carnally.

We neglected the poor.

Perhaps mounting guilt put lead in our shoes as the months passed. Our spirits flagged, and we felt like shapeless, useless blobs of clay.

Mercifully, the season of incarnation presents a time to renew hopes, revive spirits, and move beyond the failures of the past months. The year is late, but it's time to rejoice that the Lord has come:

To put the clay back on the wheel.

To mold us again.

The Author

Wally Kroeker has worked in journalism since 1967, primarily in the areas of business and religion. Earlier he worked for the *Regina Leader-Post, Winnipeg Tribune, Saskatchewan Business Journal, Moody Monthly,* and edited *The Christian Leader,* the magazine of the U.S. Mennonite Brethren Church.

Currently Kroeker edits *The Marketplace,* a magazine for Christians in business, published by Mennonite Economic Development Associates (MEDA). His freelance articles have appeared in nearly a hundred business and religious publications. He is the coauthor of *Faith Dilemmas for Marketplace Christians.*

Kroeker studied journalism at Northwestern University in Chicago and completed his undergraduate degree in religious studies at Tabor College, Hillsboro, Kansas. He has a master of arts degree in theology from the Mennonite Brethren Biblical Seminary, Fresno, California.

Current business involvements of Kroeker include serving as secretary of Kroeker Farms Ltd., a family agribusiness corporation in southern Manitoba, and as secretary of Premier International Genetics Ltd., a livestock breeding company.

Kroeker's hobbies include cooking chili, following major league baseball, and serving as a prison volunteer. Wally and his wife, Millie, have two married sons and two granddaughters. They attend the River East Mennonite Brethren Church in Winnipeg.

If you would like information
on how MEDA
(Mennonite Economic Development Associates)
encourages a Christian witness
in the marketplace,
please call 1-800-665-7026.